'CH

Timothy C. Richards

Nonfiction, 2022
Timothy C. Richards, author
All rights reserved
ISBN

Published by Xznark Press LLC, St. Louis, Mo. 63129

Xznark.com

ACKNOWLEDGMENTS

To the beautiful policewomen who entrusted me with their law enforcement experiences, thank you!

To Joann, Kathy, Isabella, Kaitlin, and Jan; I wish I would have been there to protect you.

To Andria VanMierlo: thank you for contributing your photo to the cover of this nonfiction book.

Table of Contents

INTRODUCTION

Since the inception of the cops and robber's game, both sides of the spectrum have been dominated by men, On the surface, the robbers make boatloads of cash while the cops sacrifice themselves and their families to a life of danger and poverty while living in the land of milk and honey.

For some unknown reason, the cops accept their mediocre lifestyle, work two jobs, live frugally, get freebies, and spend their off-duty time looking for cop discounts on everything from old used cars to blue jeans and shoes for their children.

Of course, their children were required to go to parochial schools. No family-loving cop would send their kid to a public school; the kid might turn out like them, working in a thankless job where they could be murdered or incarcerated at any given moment.

Given the danger and the mediocre pay the male cop endures, he is still living on a higher pay scale than most women in America. The cop/crook good old boys club was about to change.

Women were starting to apply for the job of a police officer in most major cities and counties across America. They weren't like the average male cop; punch and kick first and ask questions later. The gal cops were smart and great at taking tests.

They came to the job with enthusiasm and dedication, and they were making the same pay as the guy-cop they were riding next to in a police car. There was no glass ceiling in the St. Louis Metropolitan Police Department or the St. Louis County Police Department.

But there were problems with female police officers actually policing. Many weren't physically adept at self-defense or at arresting drunk or drugged males who refused to comply. Male cops get injured when confronted with dangerous violent criminals; female cops get injured permanently, sometimes killed or deformed. Females don't take a punch to the face or head, or a kick to the torso as well as men. Men are bigger, thicker, and accustomed to fighting.

I have partnered with several female police officers in my thirty-five years as a city cop. I was always protective of them. I respected their decision to better themselves financially, but I was skeptical of the crime-fighting street deployment of them. Some were super dedicated; all were super smart.

At the conception of this nonfiction book, I was inspired to write about a St. Louis County police officer, Sergeant Andria VanMierlo. She came to fight crime and to lock up criminals. It was her dream and she was obsessed with it. Cops examine the system and after four or five years they grow to realize the flaws in the justice system. It becomes a job, not an obsession. Not so with Andria VM. She charged ahead until the end. The idea cooked in my brain for years. We chatted about the prospect but it never came to pass. It has, now.

The concept evolved, as all creative endeavors do. There are now twenty-nine female cop vignettes in this book; some are comical, and some of the cops were killed in action. Some married cops, which in many cases is the same as being KIA. Some were promoted and took their place in the safety of a desk and prospered in the system. Some were incarcerated.

As I looked into the death of a female city cop (Kathy Censky) twenty years ago, I uncovered a possible murder of her by a member of a St. Louis biker gang in the great state of Kentucky. She was advised by her supervisors to cease and desist her association with the biker gang. She ignored the advice of her supervisors. She enjoyed riding her Harley with them. Poor choices kill cops.

The death was earmarked as an accidental death and it was never investigated. It wasn't within the jurisdiction of St. Louis, Missouri; Kentucky cops ignored the death of Officer Kathy Censky. I found discrepancies in the statements of the witnesses to her death. Her body was fleeced of her cop identification, her cash, her gun, and her badge. First responders were not advised that she was an active member of the St. Louis Metropolitan Police Department.

The cop job is a villainous demon who examines your every waking hour, looking for a chink in your armor he can work to destroy you. It will make your wife or husband a lonely person, even when you are in her presence or it can make him/ her a grieving widow/widower. Most male cops are prepared for this assault on their psyche and their bodies; few women are. The ones who fight back are bombarded with character assassination lies. Some of the cop gal's fall prey to predator ranking quid pro quo hound dog cops; wherever a dog lies they leave their hair.

It's a tough job, folks. It takes a champion to survive it; in my humble opinion, all female cops are Champs.

1

STEVE WALDMAN

The Central West End of the City of St. Louis, Missouri is the shining star of the region. Millionaire mansions, street shopping, and dining, bars, nightspots, The Chess Hall of Fame, cobblestone streets, and cul-de-sacs. It is also where visitors get raped, robbed, and murdered. But that isn't big news in St. Louis.

In the ancient eras of law enforcement, crooks and cops were basically the same, except for an oath and a badge. Both pack dwellers follow a designated leader. Not all crooks are followers; or cops, but most are. There are entitlement cop/crooks, aggressive cop/crooks, and passive cop/crooks. But the species has the hair of the dog in them. A dog will always take the winning side.

In the 1950s, 60s, 70s, and 80s there were few city cops who hadn't killed the bad guy. It was almost like joining a fraternity or going through the initiation of a good-old-boys club. Pack followers.

It's what the city fathers of the community wanted and expected. Cops don't make the rules; at the time, the State of Missouri controlled the police department through a state-appointed board called the Board of Police Commissioners. They made the rules. Blaming cops for shooting criminals is like blaming the gun instead of the shooter.

Aggressive cops impressed the commanders sitting at their desks in headquarters; shot/killed criminals impressed the commissioners. Most cops are born followers. They are distinguished by their ability to take tests and/or kill crooks.

Not just any crooks, street crooks. The Chicago Mafia had a hold on the region by controlling labor and trade unions. Nobody killed them, except their friends from Chicago and their union buddies. Cop scuttlebutt about the shooters ran rampant.

Allegedly, Lieutenant Colonel John Doherty, Chief of Detectives, shot and killed thirty criminals. Another guy, Sergeant Bob Hawkins killed twenty. I recently checked for documentation on the shootings. There is no record of them for either old deceased cop.

But many of the cops were unstable. They were never around stable people. In the old days, the station house was like an insane asylum. Crazy people coming and going, fights, prisoners being interrogated, beaten, angry cops stressed to the max, and supervisors sitting at their desks reading our reports and hardly ever leaving the stationhouse.

The only time a cop could be free of crazy people was when he was riding alone, between radio assignments. Every call consisted of an angry, crazy black person begging to be arrested, or worse, and if that happened the cop had to take the guy or gal to the crazy-house stationhouse where the other crazy/lazy supervisors sat at their desks.

So, the hierarchy, cops, commissioners, supervisors, and test-takers bombarded the street cops with orders to lock people up. People, meaning black people. It's almost all we dealt with; most of the city was/is poor black.

Guns were a big deal. We violated the civil rights of black people by pulling them over and arresting them for carrying a concealed weapon. The circuit attorney's office never issued a warrant on them, but they never got their gun back. It took a writ of replevin to retrieve the gun. They never had the cash to hire an attorney. But they could always buy another one on the street. They were Saturday night specials, trash guns made in South America.

No telling how many people I arrested for C.C.W., and how many guns I took off of the street. But if the cop wanted to be in good graces with his supervisor, he needed to get C.C.W arrests.

Anyone, twenty-one years of age, can legally carry a concealed weapon now if they aren't a convicted felon. So, for approximately fifty years, the city jails were packed with felons waiting to get out after twenty hours of incarceration, being fingerprinted, photographed, and questioned by detectives pertaining to other heinous crimes, illegally.

The Honorable Board of Police Commissioners was comprised of businessmen and lawyers. They knew what they were doing. The cop on the street took the heat for these felony violations. The arrestee had a felony arrest on their record, even though it wasn't prosecuted.

In 1978, I (cop/writer/author) was assigned to the prestigious Intelligence Unit. We spied on the Mafia, which was no big feat because they were ensconced into every form of St. Louis life. Politics, unions, drugs, burglaries, prostitution, the Chicago Mafia controlled sleepy old St. Louis, Missouri.

On a sunny October afternoon, I was swinging through the Central West End (CWE) looking for a possible CCW arrest. It was a felony arrest and would make his bosses think I was a team player, which was so far from the truth. It was like shooting fish in a barrel. The people carrying weapons knew the unmarked police cars on sight. They were identical to the other police cars in the city, except they didn't have placards or roof lights. Mine was decorated with a white stripe on the sides and fancy spoke hubcaps, but it was still a cop/car.

Guilt is something that is difficult to hide. When I would examine the drivers of the vehicles coming and going past me in traffic, I would look for the telltale sign that the driver had his gun with him on this fine day.

It happened at Euclid and McPherson, a guy in a dirty white van. He looked at me and had panic on his face. I whipped the police car around and tossed the Starsky and Hutch red light on the dash, the van pulled over.

I did my usual, "License please, where are you going, why are you here, are you strapped? Step out of the van."

The driver, Steve Waldman, a white guy, climbed out. I asked him again, "are you strapped?"

"Yes, sir,' He replied. "I have a Colt 45-caliber pistol in my belt."

"Keep your hands where I can see them," I replied. I reached under his shirt toward his waistband and felt the butt of the weapon. Certainly not a Saturday night special. I carried a Colt 45 in the Marine Corps.

"It's cocked, sir," Steve advised me.

I seized the weapon, de-cocked it, and stuck it into my waistband for safekeeping. I handcuffed Steve and placed him in the backseat of my cop/detective staff car. I was curious about why this polite hard-working guy was riding around the CWE with a cocked and loaded Colt 45. We chatted.

Steve was friends with several cops I was familiar with, and he worked near the CWE making deliveries for an auto parts store. "Why Steve," I began, "are you riding around with this weapon?"

"I am in fear of my life," he replied.

I took a long hard look at Steve Waldman. He was sincere. Most arrestees sitting in the back seats of cop detective cars with bracelets on are not. I got Steve out, returned his Colt to him, and advised him he was free to go.

Steve climbed into his van and headed north. The arrest meant nothing to me. It was a "sausage pinch", meaning it was inconsequential. It meant everything to Steve Waldman. In his mind, I spared his life.

I never could figure out why Steve was so grateful for the discretion. Cops had it back in the old days. Allegedly there is no discretion today. With cameras and microphones and citizens watching every move a cop makes, we are robots.

We remained friends, Steve, and me. He was a lead guitar player (and good) and he played in several Rhythm and Blues Bands in the Soulard area of the city. Good blues, Chicago style, were sought after in St. Louis.

I would take my wife and we would have a date night watching and listening to him and his band. Steve advised my wife that I had saved his life. I never could figure out why Steve felt this way, but I accepted his friendship which is still there today. About thirty years of loyal friendship.

We met for lunch recently, both us retired and old, and Steve felt like talking. "

"I had applied for a job with Dupont, the paint company as a sales representative," Steve began. "If you had arrested me, I wouldn't have gotten that job. The job and you saved my life."

"Okay, cool," I replied thinking that was the end of the story, but it was just the beginning.

"When I was twenty-two years old, my mom was associated with a famous lawyer, John O'Connell Hough. He was a worker's compensation attorney and he handled the worker's compensation claims for the Pipefitters local 562.

My interest was peaked; in the 60s, 70s, 80s, and 90s the local had been wreaked with Chicago Mafia killings and car bombings, shooting deaths of business agents, card-carrying members who were hitmen, diamond burglars (Jesse Stoneking), murderer, diamond thief, organized criminal, with the eastside mob.

"Lawrence Callanan," Steve continued, "the head of the Pipefitters Union was personal friends with John Hough. When a fitter was injured on the job, John Hough would file a worker's compensation case against the company the fitter was working for. It was all an insurance scheme. The companies had no say in the matter. John Hough's percentage of the take was huge. I was a card-carrying member of the union. I was taught how to weld pipes together. It could've been a good lifetime gig."

I listened while Steve continued.

"John Hough was also interested in the Dominican Republic. He and Lawrence Callanan were in the planning stage of using pipefitter pension fund money to establish a Las Vegas-style casino in Santo Domingo. There was already a casino there called The Embajabor, which was inside the Ambassador Hotel. My mom, Martha B. Waldman, gave me the job of running the casino in Santo Domingo. I knew nothing about gambling or casinos or anything else. I was twenty-two years old. But I did what my mom told me to do."

"So, your mom got her orders from John Hough"? I asked.

"Yes," Steve replied as he continued. "Eventually I was placed in and lived in a house in Miami Beach on Biscayne Bay. John Hough allegedly owned the house. He was in Santo Domingo off and on. Important people would come to the house. United States Senator Roman Hruska from Nebraska; United States Senator Tom Dowd from Connecticut; Santo Trafficante, probably the most powerful gangster in the world, controlled Florida and Cuba before the Cuban Revolution. They wanted to make The Dominican Republic another Cuba. The Mafia took a big hit when Castro tossed them out. Santo Domingo was their new target city."

"Was your mom present at the meeting?"

"Yes, the Chicago Mafia was represented by Hyman Larner, a big-time gangster from the Chicago Outfit. A guy named Ben Silverstein was with Hyman Larner. The group went to the patio and I made myself scarce. At one point I picked up a "button man" (hired killer) named Sal, with no last name, at the airport. He stayed a few days, liked the dog track and Joe's Stone Crabs, was with me the whole time he was in Miami."

I stared; Steve talked.

"Problems arose; the feds were watching anything and everything Local 562 did. There was a scheme by John Hough, Lawrence Callanan, and several St. Louis politicians pertaining to a kickback by the First United Life Insurance Company of Gary, Indiana, and the pension fund from 562. Federal Grand Juries were investigating and indictments were forthcoming. A million-dollar payoff was the prize, but Ed Henry, 562 pension representative, was indicted."

"Who else?" I asked.

"Bunch of north county cronies," he replied. Hugh Gorham, a Florissant politician was one of them. And the head of the President of First United Life Insurance Company in Indiana. Life insurance was going to be part of the pension plan for 562. The company was paying the bigshot steamfitters to use their company. It didn't work."

"So, why were you in fear?"

"Strange things started happening. John Hough disappeared. My mom felt she was in danger. I gave her a .25 automatic pistol for protection. We lived at #16 St. Alfred. Eventually, John Hough's body washed up on a beach near Key Biscayne. He'd been tortured and eventually killed. Identification had to be made by dental records. Someone had broken his leg several months before he disappeared. Big-time gangsters don't have any pity on loud-mouthed guys like John Hough. He was rude to everyone, called them names, referred to associates as nickel dime shooters, stuff like that."

"So, who do you think killed him?" I asked.

"Don't know, but we came back to St. Louis and I started carrying a gun. My mom committed suicide while talking to my dad in our driveway on St. Alfred Rd. I have never gotten over that. She killed herself with the gun I gave to her for protection. My dad never got over it either. He died shortly thereafter."

I studied Steve Waldman. Only a cop could bump into a guy with a story like this. Steve could read me. He studied me as I watched him. I was familiar with the homes on St. Alfred Road. People with cash flow lived there; professional people, doctors, lawyers, and such.

"John Hough used my mom as a front. I will never forgive him for that."

Steve and his girlfriend stayed in the family home on St. Alfred. He never knew who was going to knock on his door, follow him and shoot him in traffic, or torture him to death after abducting him. But guys like Steve, his parents, and his brothers, know about federal law enforcement agencies; they learn at an early age not to trust them.

If being interviewed by an FBI Agent, they will ask the interviewee questions they already know the answers to. They will act like they are your friend and there will always be two of them so that they can testify against you in a court of law.

Wealthy families know the law, but middle-class folks do not. Federal law, 18 USC Section 1001, lying to an FBI Agent can get you prison time. Steve grew up with this information. There was a knock on the St. Alfred door one morning. Steve cautiously went to the door, his .45 Colt automatic stuck in his waistband at the small of his back. Two guys in suits were smiling at him through the storm door glass.

"FBI", they said, holding up their credentials for Steve to see. Steve opened the door to converse.

"Are you Steve Waldman," one of them said with a smile.

"No, I'm his brother," Steve replied.

"Where is Steve?" The agent asked.

"He doesn't live here, I don't know where he is," Steve replied. The agents walked to their car and drove off. Steve Waldman was never bothered by federal law enforcement again.

2

BURGLARS & FEMALE COPS

The big crimes never stop in St. Louis. To the cop, it seemed like every person he came into contact with was a criminal, low life's on the street; and, high-class professional people. The burglary groups were busy and organized. Alarm companies were unsophisticated and technologically behind the times. It was a new field of endeavor.

Cash and diamonds were the booties of the professional burglar, and there were plenty of those commodities in most businesses in the region. Cash is king, and business owners know the value of cash, so they hide it instead of banking it.

There were several good safe crackers in the region; George Eidson was probably the best. He specialized in diamonds and cash, and he could occasionally bypass an alarm system. He got caught often but was not deterred.

A burglar, Russel G. Byers, was not as sophisticated as George Eidson, but he still made money burglarizing businesses. He had a plan to break into the St. Louis Art Museum and steal some valuable artwork.

No sophistication here, he hit the front door glass with a sledgehammer and waltzed in. There were guards on the inside, but they were in a different part of the building and didn't hear the horrendous crashing of the plate glass hitting the floor. Byers stole several pieces of art and made good his escape.

He tried to fence some of his artwork to an art restorer who had an antique shop in the Chase Park Plaza Hotel, but the fence advised him it was too specialized for him to resale. Byers had stolen a silver trophy and he showed it to the art fence. Nope, too easily identifiable. So, Byers went home and melted the trophy down to molten silver, cast it, and then returned to the fence. The fence bought it.

The Art Museum in St. Louis is cherished by most of the citizenry of the region. It is sacred ground. The city cops scrambled for information, which led them to Russell G. Byers. I had been a City of St. Louis cop for eight years.

Russell G. Byers was brought in and interrogated by city detectives. Interrogation in those ancient times usually meant being beaten with a Yellow Pages on the top of the head until the proper answers spew out. It worked every time. Most of the artwork was recovered.

But Byers was never prosecuted for the heinous sacrilegious crime. He had a story to tell, and the feds got caught up in the story and Byers was whisked away to some safe place to talk to them. The talk was about the assassination of Dr. Martin Luther King Jr. in Memphis.

Byers had stated at one time that he had been offered $50,000 by two St. Louisans, stockbroker John R. Kauffmann, and patent lawyer, John H. Sutherland, to kill King. He had testified before a federal grand jury, and he had been incarcerated with James Earl Ray, the man who confessed to the murder and then recanted.

I am using this crime, my reader friend, to emphasize the scope of crime in St. Louis in the 70s and 80s compared to the crime at this point in time. Burglars/criminals desired money. They were crooks for money, and they didn't wish to work for it, so they stole.

Today's crooks are murdering each other for a misspoken word, pride, revenge, or gossip. Many get away with the most serious crime, murder, because people in the villages they live in are afraid to give statements to the police, and I do not blame them.

Back to James Earl Ray, killer of Dr. Martin Luther King. The irony of the crime game never ceases to amaze. Irony oozes like sweat from a shirtless fat-man playing halfcourt in the summer heat. We are all so connected in a region like St. Louis. I grew up in Alton, Illinois, the hometown of James Earl Ray. He lived just blocks from where I lived.

There was a basketball court across the street from my house in the Lincoln School Grade Schoolyard. I played basketball there, and so did most kids and young adults in a ten-block radius. James Earl Ray was there a few times. He bullied young people like me, taking our basketballs and refusing to give them back, checking us and knocking us down. He went to prison and I never saw him again.

James Earl had a younger brother, Jerry Ray. He was huge, like a mutant, and he came to the basketball court a couple of times. He and his mother lived in a basement apartment of a large house that had been broken up into apartments. I had been there a few times. Jerry was a loner and didn't care about sledding, basketball, or anything else. He recognized the fact that he was a freak of nature, and he just wanted to live in the basement with his mother. He was so large that a friend and neighbor kid who was a tough guy got into a dispute with Jerry Ray. The tough kid had to jump as high as he could to sucker punch Jerry Ray in the jaw. Jerry didn't fight back.

They moved out of the neighborhood and I never saw him again. Russell Byers continued his conspiracy snitch fest with the feds, which was probably imaginary; but kept him out of prison.

I became an Intelligence Unit Detective and spied on the Mafia types in the region, females started showing an interest in law enforcement. Maybe because of television cop shows, or just the excitement of the job, but they were smart at taking tests and local police departments could not refuse them employment, so they were trained and let loose on the streets of St. Louis to ply their trade in the good old boy club, and to ride with guys like me.

Ouida Baynham, a secretary at the Nooter Corporation, desired to be a St. Louis cop. She was a reserve officer, which meant she rode in cars with cops, carried a gun and a badge and a nightstick, and basically observed what real cops do. She was a volunteer cop, without pay.

She had ridden with me on occasion. These gals could go to any district in the city (there were nine) but for some reason they wanted to ride in the bloody ninth district, the Central West End District. I had had close calls with Ouida backing me up. Street creatures are like wild animals, and they quickly sense any weakness during all combat situations. It's how they survive; combat situations arise frequently for them.

Being a City of St. Louis cop and not knowing how to fight is like being a lifeguard who can't swim.

Ouida couldn't fight, so that left the street fighting to me. It wasn't a good feeling when your supervisor advised you that reserve officer Ouida was going to be your partner. Every night was fight night.

Ouida eventually became an official City of St. Louis Police Officer. She was beaten by a man while on a disturbance call. She was in critical condition for months and was eventually given a disability retirement. She died shortly thereafter.

In 1951, several women were hired by the St. Louis Metropolitan Police Department: Winona Schrieber, Patricia Murphy, Phoebe Cribbin, Marie Moyer, Kathleen McDonald, Beatrice Obermeyer, Flora Mae Jones (first black woman to be hired), and Viola Messerli. This was also the first-time female employees (officers) were given the power of arrest and were sanctioned to carry firearms.

There isn't much data on these women police officers, but from 1971 until 1973, a Cadet, Bruce Bateman, was assigned to the seventh district detective bureau as a clerk.

In those days applicants who were not yet 21 years of age could go into the cadet program until they turned 21. They were mostly gofers, running errands for the cops in their units. Some of them drove drunk commanders around to local taverns, or drove them home in their command cars, then picked them up in the morning.

The seventh district was packed to the gills with poor blacks, but there was a small area of mansions built for the 1904 World's Fair across from Forest Park, gated and protected by private security.

A cop could walk out of the building, accidentally bump into some passerby, and if he wished, he could drag the pedestrian inside of the station and run his name, and the guy or gal would be wanted for a felony. No one in police headquarters, or anywhere else in the region cared what happened in the 7th police district.

Bruce showed up for work to the dilapidated haunted house of a building. It was a scary place. Historically, so many locals were killed, tortured or illegally incarcerated there that the building was folklore for the cops and the residents of the bloody 7th district.

One of Bruce's first assignments was to go across the street to the drug store and get Detective Marie Moyer some snuff. He noted that Detective Marie sat at her desk and smoked cigars, so he ignored the order for him to fetch her some snuff.

An old detective chastised him for not following orders. Bruce defended himself, stating that he thought they were spoofing him just to see if he would complete the chore. Bruce quickly completed the assignment and placed the snuff on Detective Marie's desk while she sat there and stared at him, smoking cigars and blowing the smoke in his face.

Detective Marie went the distance, 20 years as a city cop, and retired as a clerk in the prisoner processing division.

In your mind's eye, reader friend, compare Detective Marie to the modern policewoman on the cover of this nonfiction book, or to the other beautiful policewomen in the interior of this book. The job draws people; it's exciting and different. There's a saying in the cop game; it takes all kinds."

At about the same time period, early 1970s, the chief of police started a street crime unit called TACT, an acronym for Tactical Anti-Crime Taskforce.

The unit had its offices in the basement of headquarters. Commanders and supervisors were scrambling to get their friends assigned to the unit. It was going to be a shoot um up street crime fighting unit.

It was 99 % male cops assigned there, but one tall attractive light skinned African American cop, Cassandra Jackson, was transferred there.

She was protected by the other male cops; she was not only attractive, she was feminine, almost childishly sweet, even though she was almost six feet tall.

She hit the ground running with the male cops. They were shooting street criminals on a nightly basis; Cassandra even shot an armed robber.

She was given awards and accolades and she was adored by the black rank and file commanders. Anything she wanted she was available to achieve through her admirers.

One day, she told the commander that she desired to go back to a district, in uniform; they tried to talk her out of the decision; she held her ground.

She was placed in the 9th district, Central West End area, I was advised that I was going to be her partner. So it happened; we rode around the city and didn't speak to each other. She advised me she had never been in a car with a white man. I believed her.

By the time the night watch rolled around we were friends; we talked freely and I liked her, and enjoyed riding with her. I was protective of her; she was frightened most of the time and her demeanor brought out my primitive male side, protect the female.

We got too close; I was married with one child and had just graduated from the University of Missouri. I had worked the night watch most of the time and attended classes during the day. I felt a sense of freedom not having to do that anymore.

Cassandra had an apartment in the CWE. She invited me into her apartment while on duty. I refused to go; I waited in the parking lot when she stopped by her apartment.

I knew I was being vamped by the attractive mixed race lady cop, but our attraction for each other made the nights go by quicker.

Other cops noticed our closeness; cops observe and talk; gossip is huge in any police department. It was common knowledge that I was married, and that Cassandra was divorced.

Time marches on; we had been play-dating for several months and I knew I was being clubbed with a velvet hammer, and enjoying it.

Before one of our shifts, our supervisor, Lieutenant Buster Alphin, called Cassandra into his office. He advised her that he was going to split up our partnership.

Cassandra advised Buster that if he did split us up, she would resign immediately. Bear in mind, Cassandra could write her own ticket in the police department. Buster Alphin backed off, dismissed Cassandra and she walked out and into the report room, waiting for her partner, me.

Buster then called me into his office; "Your fucking Cassandra Jackson," he calmly said.

"No, I'm not," I replied.

"You better be careful," he advised.

"I will, Buster," I replied.

The friendship and the police work continued. We had gone through a day watch and were preparing for another date night night-watch.

We began the night watch; it was winter and in St. Louis everything is black. A night watch cop hardly ever sees daylight or white people. We were parked in a deserted neighborhood near a deserted warehouse district; rats scrambled around in the streetlights, our car was idling and the heater was putting out.

We had never made any bodily contact, not even hands, and on this night, Cassandra had a bottle of whiskey in her purse. She brought it out, opened it and poured two paper cups of it. "You've never tried to kiss me," she said. I reached for one of the cups but before I could get in my hand, a good friend cop who I had ridden with on several occasions (Fred Lengerer) pulled up to the driver's side door. I rolled down the window and smiled at him. It was always fun and games and laughs between cops, especially on winter night watch.

The police cars were almost touching he was so close. He softly said, "They're listening to you." He drove off. I took the drink from Cassandra and tossed the paper cup of booze out of the window.

"What did he say?" she asked.

"Nothing," I replied, it was a joke. I placed the police car in gear and patrolled the remainder of the shift. A few days went by and Cassandra was transferred to prisoner processing. It was apparently where she wanted to go. There's no danger there, it's warm in the winter and cool in the summer and the cops assigned there go home on time.

I would occasionally see Cassandra when I was transporting prisoners or had to go to the jail to interview a prisoner.

"I can get you assigned here with me," she would say. "We would be together again."

"No, thanks," I replied.

Cassandra's stellar reputation was being tarnished by her attitude toward her supervisors and the police department in general. She hated the job.

One day she abruptly resigned. She had some savings in the police credit union and she stormed in there demanding that she be given her savings at once.

She was advised that she would have to wait for a certain amount of time before her funds would be given to her. She ranted and raved and threatened. The credit union employees called the chief's office and they sent a high-ranking black guy down there to calm her down.

She walked out with her savings. I'd heard she got a security job, maybe at one of the casinos. Gossip reigns. I also heard that she was gambling frequently at a casino that she was not employed by, and losing.

She purchased an apartment on once prestigious Lindell Boulevard, not now, and she worked and gambled. One day she didn't show up for work; she was checked on and she was in bed, dead.

Anne Clifford came to the St. Louis Metropolitan Police Department from Olney, Illinois, home of the albino squirrels; every place is famous for something.

Anne was a domestic, helping old people and people who were disabled. The police department paid better than her previous employment, so she applied.

It's a strange process of fights; you are compelled to fight to get the job. A background check is in depth and lengthy; the police academy is a fight, especially for females who hadn't been in the military, most of the male cops had been in the Marine Corps or Army. Some Navy guys, not many Air Force recruits.

Learning to shoot a pistol was/is difficult for a female, but they all seem to get a high enough score to make it through. The city needs cops, back in 1970 when I was hired, and now.

Anne was assigned to the 9th district; I was still assigned there, even after I had gotten my bachelor's degree. I was just hanging on and out waiting for something within or without to happen.

Anne was a sweet woman. She was on my watch and she took the job seriously. She gave it her all. We hadn't ridden together and

I thought that was strange because I was almost always teamed with a female cop.

Maybe the Cassandra Jackson episode dissuaded the supervisors from placing me with gal cops. So, we didn't ride together in the same car, but we assisted each other on calls.

The crazy street people had taken over the district, and the city. Most of our radio calls were babysitting or arresting mental patients.

Anne had received an assignment to a grocery store on Lindell for a disturbance. A lady who was crippled and walked with two crutches, the kind that has handles and circular braces on them, had beaten her young son with her fists. The store manager called the police.

This crazy lady had arms like a professional wrestler, and big shoulders. She had been essentially walking with her hands and arms since puberty. Her legs didn't work.

I had the job on this fine day to drive the cruiser (paddy wagon) and Anne called for an assist and a conveyance; I got the call to assist her.

"We're taking her to prisoner processing," Anne advised. I could tell Anne was upset. Her son was probably nine years of age and his face was puffed up and bleeding. Another conveyance took him to the hospital.

The lady couldn't climb into the paddy wagon, so we turned her around, I got up on the inside and grabbed her by her arms and pulled her into the truck. I noted her muscles.

I drove her to prisoner processing, pulled into the Sally Port and Anne and (who had been riding shotgun with me) and I climbed out. The trick now was to get the muscled-up woman down and out of the truck. She was surly, cursing us as we tried to help her.

Anne was inside of the truck and I was on the ground trying to figure out how we were going to do it. The lady was partially standing with the help of her crutches, and then she leapt into the air and landed on me, full body. We both went to the hard deck and she was still on top of me. She was heavy, like a man, but crippled. I was trying to get her off of me and she didn't want to get off of me so we twisted around on the ground until I used a wrestlers move and tossed her onto her back.

Anne was laughing so hard I thought she was going to pass out. She couldn't stop laughing, and I admit it must've been comical. I jumped up and brushed my uniform off. The crippled lady just laid there on the concrete and waited for us to get her up.

Anne booked her for assault; of course, she couldn't be held so she was released back to her life on the street. I would see her occasionally; she laughed at me as I drove past her.

I was transferred to the Intelligence Unit. Anne stayed in the ninth district for years. Eventually she was transferred to the Intelligence Unit, where I was still assigned. She still laughed at me when we were together in the unit offices; she couldn't get the image of that lady jumping onto me and us going to the ground. If only it would have been video recorded.

Everyone assigned to Intelligence goes through several partners until they find one that fits their needs. Anne was no different. She finally teamed up with a hard charging cop that came to the police department to become the chief. He was the guy I refer to in this writing as the cop associated with Pipefitters Local # 562.

I'm certain Anne learned a lot from him. Tenure in the Intelligence Unit is short. I did eight years there; Anne did about the same. Her partner started making rank and eventually made it to the top. Of course, he got forced out for being a crook, but in the scheme of things he really didn't care; he got what he wanted, Chief of police and a huge pension.

I banged around the police department, detached to the Drug Enforcement Administration, Homicide Section, and then back to the ninth district. There are only good jobs in the city police department.

Anne found herself in the Sex Crimes Unit. She worked there for about twenty years. Sex crimes is actually rape, child rape, sexual deviation, incest. She was single and she emersed herself into her job.

I would see Anne occasionally and she always laughed and poked fun at me. She retired with thirty years on the police department. She got sick and died, and didn't get much of her pension.

Alana Hauck is a city girl. Like most city residents, she grew up watching and gauging the city cops. It's almost a sport in the city. The cops were always in danger, either from criminals or the police department upper echelon.

I didn't know Alana personally, but I was in the same south patrol superstation as she; Alana was in the third police district, I was in the first police district.

I noticed her because she was intense. She tried to do a good job. She was intent on promotion, like I've mentioned in this writing, the female cops wanted the power of command rank and they knew how to achieve it.

Don't use sick leave; have good stats; make your supervisor think you like him/her; score high on the promotional tests. It's a simple formula to success; many of the male cops didn't know or care about being promoted; that gave the female cops an edge.

Alana was promoted to sergeant and then lieutenant. She was a district watch commander, the person who supervises an entire staff of street police officers.

Alana was/is gay and she didn't try to hide it, although she bore two beautiful daughters. She had a gay city police officer girlfriend and they marched in the gay pride parade in (Alana) uniform held in the CWE every year.

The first time they marched, police officers who were assigned to the event stood on the sidelines and watched them. The second year they joined her in the march. City cops are easily led; they just need incentive.

Alana was loved and respected by her male/straight street cops. She respected and loved them back; she was protective of them, not from the street creatures that define the cop job, but by the ivory tower upper echelon who are always looking for some street cop to persecute.

The city workhouse was a jail in north St. Louis that housed prisoners awaiting trial, crooks who couldn't afford bail, or didn't qualify for a recognizance bond. In the city, in order to post bond on a felony, the person securing the bond must forfeit ten percent of the bond to a bail bondsman. Poor people don't have the ten percent so the arrestee sits in jail awaiting trial.

The city residents wanted that policy overturned and they wanted the city workhouse closed, so they protested. In 2017 professional protestors along with local residents embarked on a violent protest in and around the City of St. Louis, some of which was targeted near the workhouse.

City cops were deeply involved; as the protests gathered steam the protestors became violent and threw projectiles at the police trying to hold the line.

Some of the projectiles were chunks of concrete; several cops were injured by the flying pieces of concrete; Alana was struck in the shoulder.

She was treated and released but the injury never healed; it has plagued her for years. She is still fighting the injury. The life of a lady cop.

The female cops with bachelor degrees and three or four years of police experience were eligible to be hired by federal agencies; DEA, for one.

As previously mentioned, after my Intelligence Unit assignment, I was transferred (detached) to the Drug Enforcement Administration.

I eventually teamed up with Special Agent Mike Braun. Mike was on the road to success with the agency. He had graduated number one in his academy class and the DEA upper echelon were interested in him. He was an Illinois State Trooper before DEA.

In the police department everyone knows everybody else's business. It was spread around the department that I was having marital problems (true rumor) and that nasty bit of information followed me to DEA. My wife had had enough of the St. Louis Metropolitan Police Department, and me. Miraculously, we were able to work out our problems, but it took years.

To the civilian staff and female federal agents, I was labeled as fresh meat. The situation was comical at first but droned on after time. If a detached cop was interested in having an affair, DEA was the place to do it. I wasn't interested.

Mike scared up a case, and I knew the players from being in the Intelligence Unit. Paul Robinson, his brother, Dan Robinson, and a hustler named Rick Yackey.

They had been smuggling cocaine and marijuana in from south Florida for years. Paul had been incarcerated by a search warrant executed by the Hollywood, Florida police department. He got out and came back to St. Louis.

His brother Dan and Rick Yackey had been dealing in cocaine while Paul was incarcerated; they had a mule who would drive to Miami and bring back multiple kilos in the trunk of a rental car.

When Paul came back to St. Louis, he advised Dan and Rick that they owed him part of the proceeds from their years of cocaine smuggling while he was incarcerated.

He quietly advised them that if he didn't get payments from them, he would kill their children. That Paul, he's all heart.

Paul was the scum of the earth. He was basically a pimp, murderer, tough guy for the eastside mob, and drug smuggler. Nobody messed with Paul Robinson, not even the St. Louis Mafia. They came to him wanting their cut in his drug smuggling operation and he told them to fuck off. They did.

Paul ordered up tons of marijuana from a Colombian drug lord, on consignment, sold it for millions in St. Louis, and then stiffed the drug lord. Even the Colombians were afraid of Paul Robinson. After Arresting Paul Robinson (Rick Yackey set him up) I had the opportunity to convey Paul to the Federal Marshall's office in downtown St. Louis.

Paul was surly and sneered at me as we spoke, (me driving and watching him through a rearview mirror) as Paul sat in the back seat.

I mentioned to him that this was probably going to be a long sentence for him. "O, yeah," he replied. "Everybody's got to be someplace."

Since this case started in south Florida, the United States Attorney in the Southern District of Illinois (Cliff Proud, former City of St. Louis cop) where the initial seizure of the cocaine and marijuana began, wanted the south Florida DEA field office involved.

The south Florida field office (Miami) sent a female DEA agent to St. Louis to assist with the Paul Robinson et al drug case. Why she was sent was a mystery to me, but as I thought on it, I figured she might have been placed in a position to become friends with Mike Braun. He was going to the top of the drug agency; (retired from DEA as the Chief of Operations). Being friends with him could be beneficial to her. The Miami female agent was a gorgeous gal; she could write her own ticket and get anything she wanted. She rode around with me while she was in St. Louis.

I fell for hard for her. My group supervisor observed my demeanor around the gorgeous special agent, and called me into his office.

"She's the property of a Group Supervisor in Miami," he advised me. "Don't think you are going to go anywhere with her. She's taken, Capiche?"

"Sure, boss," I replied.

But at the time I was mentally belly aching about how gals like her are immediately taken by the guys in management. Group supervisors are the backbone of the agency. Their guys and gals make cases on big-time drug dealers and smugglers.

So, one day she and I talked about her life in beautiful south Florida. She told me that she and her boyfriend (group supervisor) had purchased a nice condo together and that they had a boat, a small cruiser, but they were planning on getting a larger boat, and that they travelled some and boated when they were in Miami.

I had been to Miami with my parents as a youth. We ate at some expensive restaurants, so cool that I never forgot them. I mentioned them to her and she said she and her boyfriend ate there.

I tried to add up the cost of living in Miami, with a boat, travel and eating out. It was big-time money, but I figured that with both of their salaries and overtime, maybe they could do it. Special agents get paid much more than city cops. I dismissed it.

The case droned on and we took off Paul Robinson. His brother Dan absconded and was a federal fugitive for about six months. I eventually got him.

The beautiful special agent wandered back to Miami and finally the case went to trial. Everyone was convicted, except Rick Yackey;

he was the snitch in the caper so he got a slap on the wrist. He's super rich now, living on a ranch in one of the western states. He'd been stealing from Paul and Dan for years; they knew it but couldn't prove it. Both Paul Robinson and Dan Robinson are deceased now.

While I was still assigned to the DEA Task Force (our offices were in a bank building in fashionable Clayton, Missouri) I read in the DEA news, EPIC, (El Paso Intelligence Center) that a group supervisor in the Miami Field Office was arrested for being involved in the illegal drug business. He was a dirty agent, greedy, too.

The article went on to say that his girlfriend, also a Special Agent was fired by DEA but not prosecuted. She was a sweet girl.

3

PATROLWOMAN JOHANN V. LIPSCOMBE

The City of St. Louis Police Department had a huge reputation in law enforcement and law circles. Cops in the city were referred to as "the real PO-lice." The police executives did not try to hide the fact that their cops beat people, lied on them, planted evidence, lied on search warrant affidavits, murdered them, and tossed a gun or knife next to their bodies. It's what was expected of them and if the individual cop didn't like it, he was free to quit. It was referred to as "good police work."

It wasn't like the Marine Corps. If a Marine decided he/she didn't like it anymore they would land in the brig. Although it was operated very much like the Marine Corps. The guys with rank gave the orders and then hid and giggled into their coffee cups. I often wondered how long this class persecution was going to last. It was an inside look at the control of an entire species.

In the early 70s, before computers, the regional law enforcement departments were connected by teletype machines. In the early mornings, the teletype machines would send messages to every department showing the arrest for the previous twenty-four-hour period. The machines rattled on for an hour. Specialized street unit members were required to make a felony arrest every shift. It wasn't difficult to do if the cop/detective hustled.

Surprisingly, there were very few federal lawsuits filed against the SLMPD. Few civil rights violations or civil suits. The department was under scrutiny by the feds, but mostly untouched. With the city being controlled by the State of Missouri and governed by the Board of Police Commissioners, not the mayor, or the alderman, the city slipped under the cracks and was left alone to do what it wanted. But it was watched.

The scrutiny leveled against the city gave the St. Louis County Police Department an open door to police (under the table) in any way they wished. It was squeaky clean on the surface, had money from a working population, and they paid their cops well.

The St. Louis County cops had new cars and precinct stations that were clean and cared for in shopping centers and in strip malls. Cops could park their personal cars in secured lots. But their pay was the most impressive benefit. There was an exodus of city cops to the St. Louis County Department. Most regretted the move. There was freedom and discretion here, not there.

Damaging information was leeching out of the St. Louis County Police Department. The cop on the beat is kept in the dark pertaining to any-and-all investigations. His job is to patrol and to answer the radio, nothing more. The feds began scrutinizing the County cops.

A task force was formed called The Missouri Task Force on Organized Crime. A convicted burglar, Yvonne Dietrich, was working for the feds; she was also working for Major Pete Vasel, and Captain Jack Patty. Both famous regional cops, not as famous as John Doherty, but a close second.

Cops need informants to gain a giant reputation; it's what cops desire; notoriety, fame, and then maybe money. But very few cops get rich in the cop/crook game. Catching burglars in the act inspires the public to idolize the brave cops.

Vasel and Patty dreamed up (as Yvonne Dietrich advised) a burglary at the S.F. Durst Company in Maryland Heights, Missouri, a suburb of St. Louis. Their plan was to have Yvonne set up the burglary and then have two other burglars do the heist. Patty and Vasel would be waiting for them to exit the building and they would capture them.

The chemicals stolen were used to make Methamphetamine. Yvonne Dietrich was going to get half of the stash from the St. Louis County Police Department. The operation was okayed by the upper echelon of the County Police Department. It also was deemed "good police work".

The original burglars Dietrich had hired for the job failed to show up, so she contacted two other thieves to do her bidding: Paul Williams and Larry Smith. They broke in and as they were leaving, they were arrested. Job well done. The owners of S.F. Durst Chemical Company were out a load of dope, but they didn't complain.

Yvonne Dietrich was arrested by the feds and she spilled her guts. She'd been giving bribes to city police officers also. When stopped for an investigation, her favorite line was, "I can make your dreams come true." The conversation usually went her way after that.

In 1970 St. Louis County advertised nationwide for applicants to become the new chief of police. The city has the same procedure, but it's a joke, they always hire within. An outsider wandering into the chief's position in the city would be eaten alive. They eat their homeboys after they torture and quarter them.

The county hired Robert Digrazzia, a guy who was a police sergeant in a northern California town. He was a showman who made certain everyone observed his sidearm while he spoke. He was the "ax man" for the county cops. Vasel and Patty were harassed and eventually suspended. Chief Digrazzia was the chief for approximately two years and faded away.

Of course, Vasel and Patty got their jobs back. While they were off duty they wrote a fiction book together, "Killer Cops." Allegedly about John Doherty and the bevy of killer cops patrolling the streets of the City of St. Louis.

In 1991, Johann V. Lipscomb, a beautiful and talented young policewoman, was patrolling the county roads and streets in the First Precinct. That's north St. Louis County, which at one time was the creme de la creme of places to live in the St. Louis region.

It's where the city white people fled when their neighborhoods were blighted by the federal government and turned over to the city's poor blacks. They were deemed unlivable by white people. They fled to north county.

Neighborhoods change quickly in the St. Louis region. It only took twenty-five years for the north county to become predominantly black. The white folk fled to St. Charles County, Missouri. By 1991, the white exodus was in full swing.

Johann was patrolling in the dark, alone, when she observed a person walking on the side of the road. In her mind, the walker was suspicious. She stopped her patrol car and walked toward him. It is unknown what transpired after the initial contact, but the road creature pulled a gun and shot her in the abdomen. She went down, the walker calmly walked away.

It was big news and the investigation was frantic. Residents of the suburb were already upset that they couldn't even go to the supermarket without being harassed, threatened, or assaulted by an angry black person.

The police work in the investigation was impeccable. A man named Blackmon was arrested. The weapon used to murder Patrolwoman Lipscomb was recovered. It belonged to the suspect's dad, a City of St. Louis Police Captain. Life and death on the streets and roads of the St. Louis region.

4

Intelligence Unit Detective Patty Rice

Back in the dark ages of police work, Internal Affairs would seek out cops who had just graduated from the police academy and attempt to recruit them as snitches against other cops. When they were approached, the IAD Captain would describe the proposed assignment as an undercover position to rid the police department of crooked cops. They were looking for spies.

I doubt the internal affairs scummy hierarchy were ever successful in their attempts to recruit spies, but for some unknown reason, the fact that an officer had been approached for such an assignment was a monkey on his/her back for their entire career. It happened to Patty.

A group of cops were congregating in a tavern on duty and they were caught. Patty was assigned to the same watch and the cops, who generally take things at face value, suspected she snitched on them.

Suspicion is like a wild fire, especially when it pertains to cops. Patty was ostracized, her life was in danger. She was transferred to the Intelligence Unit, the Chief's private unit where the detectives work secretly and only answer to the chief of police.

Patty was no babe in the woods; she came to the police department with a degree in English and a lot of hard time experiences. She was a bartender.

Cute and petite, she swaggered with the best of the secret unit detectives. She was Medal of Valor recipient, the highest award the St. Louis Metropolitan police Department offers brave cops.

She caught the Bionic Bandit, an escaped murderer who settled in St. Louis and robbed banks for money and fun. George Venegoni was with her. Gary Knight helped George apprehend him.

Patty and I teamed up occasionally; we worked the Synagogue sniper case; Joseph Paul Franklin was travelling around the country sniping at Jews, blacks, and liberals.

Patty worked big cases. She worked undercover for the FBI, posing as the wife of one of the agents, buying merchandise stolen in burglaries around the nation. It was organized crime; it was everywhere in the St. Louis region in the 50s, 60s, 70s and 80s.

The boss of the unit was Captain Bud Ninteman. He liked Patty. He was infatuated with her and would stake out her house in south city and spy on her.

It seemed that most of the detectives in the Intelligence Unit were seeking promotion. When a guy or gal is assigned to Intel 210 it is akin to the Mafia making someone a "made" guy.

You're trusted but watched. You are expected to do what the boss tells you to do without questioning the order. It's heady stuff for a cop. It causes turmoil within the unit and if the cop is married he/she carries it home, causing turmoil on the home front. The mantra is; Don't get transferred out without a promotion. If you do, you have failed.

Some cops get enough of the spy versus spy routine. We spied on the Italian Mafia, the Syrian Mafia and the eastside Mafia. All were politically connected.

The Italian Mafia (Chicago Outfit) controlled the two labor unions (110, and 42), and as I noted at the beginning of this book, Pipefitters Union 562.

Out jobs as Intel 210 detectives, was to spy on the organized criminals and to document their activities. Patty, me, and the other detectives did what were told and enjoyed every minute of it.

Captain Bud was unrelenting in his pursuit of Detective Patty Rice. He had been a ranking cop for 25 years in an old-fashioned police department where guys like him dated married civilian employees, and female cops. They were rarely turned down.

The Chief of Police dated young wives of cops. If the cop didn't raise a fuss, the chief would get him a job in a detective bureau, and ultimately have him promoted to sergeant.

Patty Rice rebuffed Captain Bud's advances. He finally advised her that if she slept with him, he would have her promoted to sergeant.

Patty's reply was, "Promote me first."

Captain Bud was furious; he transferred Patty back to uniform. But that was just a surface demotion. Like the Mafia, made men don't live long after they fall from grace. There was a department hit placed on Patty Rice.

They weren't going to kill Patty in the old fashion way, shooting, suffocation, knife in the back, car bombing, or thrown out of a window; they were going to give her to a supervisor who had instructions to weed her out of the department. If a supervisor hates one of his/her underlings, life becomes not worth living.

Going from a unit like Intelligence, where you are important, free to do whatever you wish, work your own hours, drive a department unmarked car and allowed to swagger around headquarters in jeans and a polo shirt, and then forcefully being transferred to a uniform district, where everything you do is monitored, you must go to roll call, fight drunks, get hurt, pick up dead bodies, have insane street people get in your face and scream obscenities at you, is a life changing experience.

It happened to Patty Rice, smart award-winning organized crime investigator. She knew every organized crook in the United States and could pick them out of a crowd at the airport, coming or going. All for naught; she slid into the blue uniform and reported to a district, there were nine of them at this time in the police department life, not that many now.

The onslaught began. Her supervisor hated her and did everything he could to make her miserable existence more miserable. Patty had a quick lip and she defended herself as best she could, but the momentum was against her. Everything she said and did was noted for future reference.

Patty's wrist was broken on a fight call. She wished to recuperate at home, but that wasn't an option offered to her. There were words thrown around and Patty was subsequently suspended.

Patty hired a lawyer and a board trial was scheduled. Board trials are kangaroo courts. They don't exist anymore because the department is being controlled by the city civil service commission. There is no Board of Police Commissioners.

The trial began and the supervisor stated his case why Patty Rice should be terminated from the police department. Patty's lawyer placed Patty's mother on the stand.

Cops at times have had witnesses try to defend them; priests, preachers, school teachers, victims they have helped in the past, but a female cop's mother is a rarity.

Patty's mother was questioned by Patty's attorney about Patty's past and future. Her broken wrist was still giving her problems and she was unable to defend herself on the street.

She was cross examined by an attorney for the Board of Police Commissioners. He mentioned that Patty spoke vulgarly to her supervisor and in general conversation.

Patty's mother stated that she didn't speak that way before she was a cop and she must have picked up that habit while employed by the police department.

The wheels were starting to turn in Patty's favor again. After much deliberation, Patty was given a disability retirement. She quickly moved to the Great State of Florida and set up residence in the southwest part of the state.

Patty won!

5

SHELLEY O'SULLIVAN

MISSIONARY; POLICE DETECTIVE

Shelley was different than the other cop gals; she was deep and intelligent, talented, and yes, attractive. But her life had been different. She grew up in Ferguson, Missouri, an infamous North St. Louis County town that would change the world of law enforcement forever.

Her happiness in life was when she was in church or playing guitar and singing. A neighbor taught her to play. Her ambitions in life were to sing and play and write music.

At age fourteen she worked at a boat harbor near a cabin her parents owned. She pumped gas, worked in the kitchen, and waited tables. She hated school and in the eleventh grade, she quit school and started a band with two other girls. They called it "Pussy Cats" and they played cover songs in local clubs and Holiday Inns across Illinois and Missouri. She loved life. She spent a lot of time in her parent's basement meditating.

She was composing in the basement and praying, writing down her thoughts; all of her lyrics were thanking God for her life. A feeling came over her, like warm honey being poured over her; she began to speak in tongues. She understood that she was talking to God. She says she was born again and surrendered herself to the Holy Spirit. She continued to speak in tongues but not in the presence of anyone.

She reevaluated her life and got a GED high school equivalency diploma and attended a bible college. In 1986, at age twenty-nine, she graduated from Life Christian Bible College. She was fixated on the Country of India and was certain God was advising her to go there.

She found a nonprofit organization called Praiseway World Missions and began to raise money for mission work in India. She went to India with her associate pastor, Jack Harris, his wife Sherry, and their two young children.

They flew into Madras, halfway down the east side of the continent, and began their ministry. They slept wherever they could; lived on rice and knew that God would provide for them. Their mode of transportation was walking.

Jack held services in open fields; it was forbidden to practice Christianity so gatherings had to be spontaneous. People came to hear the gospel; a stage was built, speakers showed up, Shelley played guitar and sang, she spoke to the masses with the microphone, never afraid; the government never tried to stop them.

Shelley's visa expired and the trip came to an end; she loved India and missionary work. She wanted to raise more money to return to India. She sang and played guitar in a St. Louis ministry; the associate minister there was the famous Joyce Meyer; Shelley composed Christian songs and produced a Christian album, "I have a dream" which was released in 1986. She was confident she would raise enough money to return to India.

This time she flew into Bombay on the west side of India. She was on her own, unafraid, and knew that God would lead her to the right people. She met a native family and eventually moved in with them. They walked into villages and acted as interpreters for her. Shelley stayed five months on this trip; she loved her life.

Her parents had moved to St. Charles County and she moved in with them again; she got a job in a grocery store. Mostly she roamed the aisles looking for shoplifters. She made enough money to return to India; she played guitar and sang in larger venues in India and she had a following of Jesus supporters.

Shelley became friends with a fourteen-year-old girl in the family she was living with; the girl wanted to come back to the United States with Shelley; the girl's dad approved and Shelley brought the girl back with her to her parent's house in St. Charles County.

Shelley was now in her thirties; she desired to be self-reliant; she saw an advertisement in the St. Louis Post Dispatch stating that the St. Louis Metropolitan Police Department was searching for police officer candidates. It's the way it happens to most of us (cops) an advertisement or commercials on television, a challenge or adventure, something new and exciting. Curiosity kills the cat, but it never stops the flow of applicants for the cop job. She was hired as a Probationary Police Officer and went into the police academy.

The police academy was a different way of life for her. For male cops, it isn't a big deal to shoot guns, fight, drink beer after class, smoke cigarettes in the hallways, or flirt with every female within arm's length.

Shelley, for her lifetime, had been loving everyone unconditionally, listening in silence, and trusting God to lead her; things were totally abstract in the cop world. She found she couldn't trust the other cops; "They were backstabbers," she replied. (Crooks Kill, Cops Lie, xznark.com, nonfiction). The police department is like a large parochial grade school; everybody knows everyone's business, weaknesses, family background, and strengths. The masses attack your weaknesses and despise your strengths. St. Louis cop 101.

Shelley was assigned to the fourth police district (downtown St. Louis) which is probably one of the plum assignments in the city. Someone was impressed with her, but intelligent attractive female cops are noticed more than male cops (fact of life).

Shelley was in the fourth district for approximately three years, the exact time the special orders of the department dictate how long a cop must serve in the department before being transferred to a specialized unit.

Violent crime is prevalent in the City of St. Louis, and it always has been. There is no utopia anywhere in The United States of America, although cops convince themselves that if they could just move to another part of the country, they would seize utopia. I always thought the State of Florida was a utopia; I worked toward moving there; it was a dream that would never come to fruition.

There is always a new specialized unit being formed in the city. So many cops have influential friends and relatives, and the chief's office is bombarded by politicians demanding that their friends be promoted or given plush jobs.

In 1993, a new unit was formed titled, Violent Crime Task Force. These specialized units make the ordinary officers, superheroes, in their minds. They overextend themselves because they feel this is their big chance to show that they are promotable.

Again, Levis and Polo shirts are the uniforms, undercover cop cars are the chariots they ride in to do superhero feats. Couple this with an attractive female cop as a partner, and you have the recipe for extreme danger.

Shelley was assigned to the new Violent Crime Task Force. Her partner was Bob Ogilvie, a hard-charging journeyman cop. Being assigned to the unit was actually a promotion of sorts. Shelley's training officer, Tom Toretta, who had been on the police force for about ten years, and desired to go to a specialized unit, was put-out that Shelley accomplished this goal and he didn't.

The police department pays for officers to attend college. It's a perk that is difficult to pass on. Shelley attended Stirling College (a school I had never heard of) and eventually graduated with a B.S. in Criminal Justice.

The cop job is full of small successes; college, arrests, specialized units, plainclothes assignments, take-home department cars, and letters of commendation from the chief; all made possible to spur the cop on to do the impossible; control crime in the murder capital of America. It sounds mundane but it is so intelligently laid out and dictated that the cop doesn't know or care that he's playing with his life and his partner's life. Cops in specialized units will do anything to remain there.

On April 15, 1993, Detectives Bob Ogilvie and Shelley O'Sullivan were riding in the seventh police district. It's the busiest district (or it was in the 90s). It's in the far western section of the city, predominantly black and poor, and no one in the city, state, or world cares what goes on there. Crime is a sport; children there grow up training to be criminals.

"The mission of the Violent Crime Task Force is to interrupt street crime", the Chief of Detectives at that time stated (Captain Dave's mentor from the Jan Fore chapter) stated.

Shelley and Bob Ogilvie were patrolling in the Kingsbury Street area of the seventh district because of recent street robberies. Street robberies were so prevalent that if you walked on the street in the seventh district your chances of being robbed were at approximately 90%.

It was about 11:30 at night and they spotted four guys standing around on the street. They decided to stop and question them; they jumped out of the detective car and said "PO-lice"; the guys ran off. Bob pursued them on foot while Shelley got back in the detective car and tried to head them off.

Bob Ogilvie cornered one of them at the rear of a vacant building, and the gunbattle began. Shelley heard several shots and as she approached, she too was fired on. Bob Ogilvie was shot in both legs; he shot at the assailant fourteen times with his nine-millimeter Beretta semi-automatic pistol. A suspect was arrested a block or so away.

Shelley and Bob Ogilvie received a Chief of Police Letter of Commendation for their heroic deeds. So, Shelley had been tested under fire; she met the criteria for better assignments.

Shelley was unavailable to her friend from India; the girl returned to India after her visa expired. "I began to realize that I went from everyone loving me in India, to everyone hating me in the police force in just a few short years," Shelley commented. But someone someplace liked her, she continued to get good assignments.

The police department has options for the chosen few. FBI Task Force, DEA Task Force, IRS Task Force. These are soft clothes plum assignments that pay more, provide a car, and are super interesting. Shelley was transferred to DEA. The same agency and the same bank building in fashionable Clayton, Missouri that I had been transferred to several years earlier. The financial district of the region. It was and is heady stuff.

The DEA Task Force assignment requires all of the cop/agent's time. DEA becomes your life, accept it or ask for a return to the police department. But in the mind, of most cops, anything is better than answering radio assignments in a district. That is the ax specialized units hold over your head.

Shelley, like most of the detached cops, landed in the federal system seeking a compatriot. In the beginning, the position is lonely and uncomforting. The cop is on his/her own and the only thing that will save them is a friend or a case. Federal cases don't just materialize out of dust on the cop's federal desk; they have to be dug for, brought to life, nurtured and protected, and eventually prosecuted.

At DEA, there are lots of male cops and not very many female cops. Shelley going there was probably a cop experiment. There was a cop assigned there who had just split with his wife. He was the chief's oldest son, Mark Scheetz.

He married a gorgeous Irish cop gal, Gwen Kavanaugh. She had grown up in and around the police department. Her dad was a career cop, and Gwen came to the department with a master's degree (by osmosis) in the SLMPD. She was hip and she was smart.

The chief, Bob Scheetz, insanely intense and unpredictable, liked Gwen Kavanaugh, she was that cute, and he was hoping that she and his son Mark would get back together. The problem was that Mark had a drinking problem. He was drunk most of the time.

Mark's nickname was Barney. He was named after a country cop in a television series, The Andy Griffith Show, who was only allowed to have one bullet, Barney Fife, who was played by Don Knotts. Mark looked like Barney Fife, and he acted like him at times. He didn't object to being called Barney.

Mark subsided on alcohol and junk food. Ballpark nachos were a staple for him, so long as they were washed down by ten-beers. He was a nice guy, just reeked from alcoholism.

Gwen, Barney's wife, was so smart and so well-liked by the chief, that she was going to be sent on a trip for some special training. An old cop, probably twenty-five years older than she was going with her. Bob Scheetz instructed the old cop to watch over her. He said he would. They became an item, eventually married and she had his son.

Gwen was promoted three times, and retired at the rank of captain. Her husband (not Barney) died early in their marriage. She received his pension as a survivor benefit while being a cop. She retired after a long career and at this time receives her pension and her deceased husband's pension. She's a wealthy gal and still cute.

Shelley dated Barney (Mark Scheetz) for several years while assigned to the DEA Task Force. It worked out for her; she survived the turmoil of the event. Mark was eventually promoted to sergeant and transferred back to the police department. He struggled as a supervisor and continued over-indulging. He took a medical leave and checked in to an alcohol rehab center. He was with street-people, the types of street-vagrants cops deal with on a daily basis.

He came back to work and started drinking again. He eventually checked back into another rehab center, took early retirement from the police department, and went into a long-term alcohol rehab center, then into a nursing home. He died of a stroke several years later.

Shelley rotated back to the police department and was placed in the homicide section. There's always an opening in homicide. It's where cops with friends get dumped; nobody survives homicide.

The Task Force is a three or four-year break from the political pressure of the police department. The rat race is so fast and intense that the cop actually believes he/she is a federal agent. The federal prosecutors befriend the cop; he hobnobs with the agents and the Assistant United States Attorneys. They eventually treat him/her as an equal, a hero who has brought them good prosecutable cases that will enhance the careers of the prosecutor. Once the cop is no longer in the federal picture, he's overlooked; not forgotten, but not viable to professional standards.

Feeling important is another deadly sin of the average everyday cop just trying to survive. After one of the prestigious task force assignments, the cop returns to the police department tainted, spoiled and confused. They're still hated by their supervisors and their peers; nothing changes in their absence from the bump and grind of being a city cop. The only true heroes (in cops' minds) are the supervisors and the ass-kissing friends of the supervisors.

Shelley hated homicide; it was time for a reevaluation of her life; she had veered off of her life path; she handed in her resignation and chalked up the nine years as a City of St. Louis cop as an adventure that had run its course.

Shelley purchased a home in Nashville, Tennessee, got a job as a courier, and wrote music after work. Open mic night was a big deal for someone starting in the music business in Nashville. She joined music writing clubs and met people in the business.

A producer collaborated with Shelley and another performer; they started a group, Blonde on Blonde, which toured in Norway for four months. She returned to Nashville and played in clubs.

She was introduced to Jean Fountain, "Our connection was immediate and I had a deep feeling that we would be soul-mates."

Blonde on Blonde played in Miami Beach, Shelley felt Miami Beach was where she belonged; she and Jean Fountain purchased a house there. Shelley was at work on April 18, 2000, when she had an aneurysm. She passed out and didn't regain consciousness for three weeks. She blamed the stroke on the homicide section.

In the fall of 2001, she and Jean Fountain moved to Point Clear, Alabama. Shelley is alive and well, living in a beach house in Alabama and trying not to remember the St. Louis Metropolitan Police Department.

Excerpts of this writing were taken from a memoir dictated by Shelley and written by Tamlin Allbritten titled, "I HAVE A DREAM---- The story of my life....(I think)."

6

Medical Examiner Rose Green & Sergeant Jeffrey Kowalski

Jeff, a hard-charging city cop, was assigned to the Mobile Reserve Unit of the city police. They didn't handle radio assignments, they patrolled the districts in uniform, in placarded cop cars with lights on top, stopping pedestrians and cars, assisting on traffic details, and basically taking the call pressure off of the district cops. They worked city-wide, and there was some freedom in their cop/job.

His partner was Patrolman Matt Rodden, and they were patrolling in the wild west seventh district, a mostly black neighborhood in the far western boundary of the city with armed street criminals roaming freely.

They were on foot, on February 19th, 1987, searching for a street creature who had robbed someone at gunpoint in the 5000 block of Vernon, a street that has always been rough, even in the early 1900s when The City of St. Louis was the epitome of cool. They split up, Kowalski and Rodden, and as luck would have it, Jeff jumped the robber, later identified as Terrell Robinson, sixteen years of age, still armed and dangerous.

Robinson ran, Jeff ran after him, Robinson turned and fired his pistol at Jeff; Jeff returned fire striking Robinson. Jeff was hit in the abdomen causing severe injuries to his pancreas, liver, and stomach. The bullet also hit his inferior vena cava, the vein that carries deoxygenated blood from the lower part of the body to his heart. Robinson was subsequently captured near the scene. He was tried as an adult and given a life sentence. He is still incarcerated.

Warriors, doctors, and old cops are aware of the ramifications of "gut shots." In most cases, it is a death sentence, but the problem is, in these days of modern medicine, the victim and the doctors think there may be a long shot to recovery through surgeries; lots of surgeries.

In the old wars, gut shot victims usually requested a coup de gras. We are civilized now, a little, anyway, so we allow the victim and his or her kin to wait and watch as the surgeries occur, the victim dwindles away in pain, and eventually dies a torturous death.

Jeff was married to Rose Green Kowalski at the time of the shooting. Rose worked at the city morgue and was the chief investigator for the medical examiner. The office manager of the morgue was Baxter Leisure, a cousin to the notorious Paul, David, and Anthony Leisure, gangsters, murderers, and bombers. Anthony is still incarcerated for the bombing of another Syrian faction gangster, Jimmy Michaels.

Jimmy's kin blew up Paul but didn't kill him instantly. He died in a federal prison hospital, blown up by a rushed attempt to bomb his car. The bombing blew Paul Leisure's leg off, and cop/gangster/gossip has it that the leg is still in the morgue cooler.

The morgue has always been a patronage/local election gig. Helen Taylor was the coroner for the city of St. Louis for decades. Her brother was an oaf but was promoted several times in the political police department due to the politics of his sister. Both are deceased.

In the little community of St. Louis, little because the taxpaying section of the city is in the southern portion of the berg, and that's where the attention remains concerning power and money. The Leisure' lived south, they had powerful relatives, just like Coroner Helen Taylor. The morgue switched from a coroner position to a medical examiner position, which meant it wasn't as powerful, but still patronage.
Baxter Leisure, who worked at the morgue at a young age, hung in and maintained the supervisory job at the morgue.

Normal, everyday working-class people were terrified of the Leisure family. Not all of them were killers or gangsters. At the morgue, where Rose Green Kowalski spent thirty-seven years of her life, daily communications between her co-employees consisted of good morning and good evening. It was a survival existence.

The Leisure family had other positions in city government. Baxter's sister worked as the office supervisor in the City Counselors

Office. They were sprinkled around in offices and getting patronage pay.

As a casual observer who didn't grow up in St. Louis or attend parochial schools with the gangster's relatives, I understood why the State of Missouri controlled the St. Louis Metropolitan Police Department.

But that plan didn't work for them. As described in chapter one of this book, state legislators from the southern parts of the city put pressure on the chief of police to promote their friends and relatives. Our pay raises had to be passed by the state legislature. State representatives would scramble to be on those committees. It was a patronage mess.

The City of St. Louis now controls the St. Louis Metropolitan police department; it's the worst mess. The City of St. Louis Mayor, who at this point in time is Tishaura Jones, is left-wing and anti-police. Her dad is Virvus Jones. He was the comptroller for the City of St. Louis in the 1990s. He went to prison for fraud and corruption. The beat goes on in old St. Louis.

There's a 500-million-dollar government gift coming to the City of St. Louis. The politicians are beside themselves trying to figure out what they are going to spend it on. Hopefully, the feds are watching and waiting.

"On the day Jeff was shot," Rose continued with our conversation, "I had gone to the hospital after being summoned by the Chief's office. I was waiting and in fear. I'd been around hundreds of gut-shot victims. Jeff and I were both young, in our twenties, just starting our careers. I knew things were bad and not going to get any better for Jeff, or me. Whatever happens to a city cop also happens to his wife."

"I understand," I replied.

"While I was waiting, Bill Bryan from the Globe-Democrat Newspaper called the hospital and wanted to interview me. I'd known Bill Bryan for years, everybody in law enforcement knew him. He liked cops; he wrote crime stories for the newspaper. I refused to speak with him. I'm a private person. I don't like being in the presence of people. I like being left alone."

"What better place to be than the morgue," I responded. She stared at me.

"Jeff was hospitalized for two months," Rose continued. "When he came home, we were distanced. The shooting was very destructive to our marriage. Jeff's personality changed. I didn't know who he was. He wasn't invested in our marriage anymore, just himself. We were only married two years when he was shot. Can you just leave me out of your book, please? I'm a private person. I don't want to bring back the past."

"No, Rose."

7

Kiki And Leadbelly

Jeff Kowalski and Rose divorced. He was a young (still in his twenties) hero cop in the City of St. Louis, Missouri, where, on the south side, cops are revered by people who work for a living. Jeff was eventually transferred to the Homicide Section, which made him more of a high-profile single cop. Crime is a team sport in cities like St. Louis. The fans know the players by name and what they've accomplished. Surprised there aren't playing cards with their names, faces and resumes on them being traded among admirers.

Ben Thomas, the founder of The Evening Whirl Newspaper, a St. Louis paper about criminals and cops with photos and vignettes, roamed the headquarters building looking for information. He spent a lot of time in the Homicide Section offices. The detectives there liked him, and he liked them. He gave them nicknames and referred to them in his newspaper by their real names and their nicknames in parenthesis. Ben named Jeff Kowalski, "Leadbelly."

The cops and the onlookers like Ben Thomas know about gut-shot victims. Jeff was offered a disability pension by the department. That would have been seventy percent of his base pay for life, but no cost-of-living-clause. A regular service pension offers seventy-five percent of your base pay and a thirty-percent cost of living benefit. Jeff chose not to take the disability.

Jeff was happy in Homicide. In St. Louis, like most democratically controlled major cities in the United States, people shoot first and ask questions later. It's a busy, frantic way to make a living. Jeff started having abdomen problems but didn't complain. Ben Thomas should have named Jeff, "Ticking Time Bomb In Your Belly."

Jeff had a flat apartment on the southside, 5007 Mandel second floor, a bachelor pad for the free guy. He shopped at the Schnucks Grocery Store within walking distance. A super cute girl, Kimberly Bates lived in the same building at 5005 on the first floor. She worked for the St. Louis County Government as a civilian employee, and also had a part-time gig at the Schnucks Grocery Store.

Kimberly liked the pseudonym, Kiki. Her disabled brother couldn't pronounce her name, so he called her Kiki. Her dad, she advised, did nothing for the family and she did not like the name Bates. It reminded her of pain and sorrow.

Kiki and Jeff had a brief conversation during a snowstorm in December of 1988. Jeff came through her line and she eventually invited herself to his solo barbeque. Kiki desired to be a City of St. Louis Cop. Another Intelligent, attractive, athletic young woman taking the plunge and coming into law enforcement.

Kiki graduated from the St. Louis Metropolitan Police Academy in May of 1990; Jeff proposed to her on stage during the ceremony; they were married in September 1991. Things started happening. Kiki was sent to the bloody third district. Again, it was like going to work in an insane asylum, just like every other district station. There were nine, and they were all the same.

The streets were filled with criminals, robbers, prostitutes, and the small percentage of citizens who weren't crooks or kooks griped to the district commanders of the crime on their streets. There were prostitutes walking around with their shirts pulled up showing their breasts trying to entice "Johns" to stop and rent them.

Someone decided that there wasn't much that could be done about the prostitutes. It was the city of St. Louis (municipal) charge, like getting a speeding ticket, and most of the girls paid the fine and then returned to the streets. It's where they got their money to buy drugs.

None of these girls were cute. They were junkies. Besides earning money for their drug habit, a lot of them were excited about being around men. It was usually their only semi-romantic experience in life. A guy paying them for sexual gratification was positive for them.

A plan was devised decades earlier, when policewomen were few and far between, and not attractive, that these young and attractive new breed policewomen should be used as decoys to trick and arrest the "Johns".

So, they put Kiki on the streets in the southside area and she walked and waved and strutted. The "Johns" would stop for her, and she would talk with them. They would ask her name and she would say "Kiki" and they would think she said "Kinky" and they would swoon over this cute new street girl who was no doubt super kinky.

The street girls are wired for sound. There are usually two big street cops hiding nearby, and they would swoop down on the perverted "Johns" and pull them out of their cars, cuff them, and take them away. Their cars would be towed, which in St. Louis means the chances of ever getting them back were slim. Organized criminals operated the city tow lots. If they can hold onto the car for a certain period of time, they can do a little paperwork with the State of Missouri and keep the car. Always a big problem for the City of St. Louis.

Of course, the tow lot crooks would give cars to their cop friends, or sell them at a ridiculously low price. But most of the towed cars were sold for a huge profit. They were gotten for nothing and sold for big cash. Such is life in the City of St. Louis.

A cute cop-gal can only do the undercover work for a short period of time. They get burned; crooks and "Johns" communicate. Soon gals like Kiki were ignored. She was thrown back into the washing machine of the street cop; answering the radio and fighting insane people.

Kiki left the police department in 1996. By then she and Jeff had two daughters; Jeff was having extreme health problems. Kiki took a job at City Hall working through a Department of Justice Grant building safety measures for city children. She worked the DOJ Grant until 2000.

Jeff took an early full disability retirement which gave him seventy-five percent of his final salary. No one could live on that but there are other perks for retired cops. They get a lump sum of other money, sick leave, etc. So, the cop going out has some cash as a buffer. The family moved to Texas. Jeff's health problems continued; he spent fifteen years dying on duty.

Jeff was diagnosed with inoperable cancer a few years later. Cancer attacked his pancreas. Kiki was fighting battles for survival for her and her two daughters. Jeff's death was imminent.

She fought with workers' compensation and she was fighting with the police pension fund to classify Jeff's pending death as line-of-duty. Jeff's doctor wrote a letter to the pension board explaining that the damage to Jeff's internal organs was caused by the bullet.

The pension board made Jeff's injury line-of-duty. Jeff passed away. In a line-of-duty death, the region's Backstoppers take over and assist the family. Kiki gets a widow's benefit from the pension fund, Backstoppers assists and takes care of any outstanding bills, and also takes care of the officer's children.

Kiki fought the system and won. She is a fighter of causes. She's still fighting, trying to be able to cast a vote during pension changes. In Kansas City, Missouri, widows of slain police officers are allowed to vote at pension board meetings.

Widows of slain police officers are also allowed to remarry and keep their pension benefits. In St. Louis, if a widow remarries, she loses her widow benefit. It isn't that way in Kansas City, Missouri.

Kiki is still fiery and cute, living a good life, tending to her children and grand-children, wearing nice clothing, and driving nice cars. She's a born fighter of causes.

8

LARRY JOHNSON

MEETS

DETECTIVE PEGGY

The sexual mores of St. Louis society have always amazed me. The Grand Burlesque in Downtown St. Louis provided nudity, along with comedy for anyone who could put their cash on the ticket counter back in the 50s. At age sixteen, I was a customer, frequently.

Street prostitutes are available in certain neighborhoods. The Gas Light Square area offered girls of every shape and color on the Stroll from Vandeventer to Newstead.

I was assigned the stroll area as a cop in 1970. We (cops) learned to not hate the prostitutes, but to hate the pimps. It was an easy thing to do. Pimps preyed on the girls and the customers. They were and are the filthiest creatures on earth.

But the hookers learned from their pimps and were just as evil given the opportunity to commit evil deeds. If there was an opportunity to steal or take advantage, the hookers did it. The trick, or John, would call the police and someone like me would get the radio assignment to meet him.

The trick was always drunk or drugged, married but not embarrassed, and belligerent. The cops knew all of the girls, we'd arrested them dozens of times. It's not a crime to be a prostitute; it's an infraction, but the captain of the 9th district, Captain Harry Lee, demanded that the hooker girls be booked, taken downtown to prisoner processing and processed accordingly. It was a twenty-hour day off for the girls. They'd be back in a day or two, walking, waving, baring their breasts. The tricks never stopped coming. That was life on the streets in the fine City of St. Louis. Pimp, whore, trick, cop.

I often wondered what made the tricks continually return to the street girls. How much sex does a man need? What are they lacking in their lives that makes them risk life and limb, and health, to pay for sex from a street prostitute? Some of the tricks were beaten by the pimps, or murdered by night ghouls who lurk in the darkness for a chance to kill just for the sport of it.

The girls were all over the city, strolls on south Broadway, downtown strolls, north city strolls. But I wasn't new to the hooker game. I'd seen it in California, Japan, Okinawa, Taiwan, The Philippine Islands, Hong Kong, anywhere there is a group of men needing sexual gratification. The street hookers weren't (for the most part) attractive, or clean. They were street people, dirty, unkempt, stinking. One step up from homeless, but they didn't live on the street, they just worked it.

The art of prostitution was different in St. Louis County. The beautiful county cop girls didn't work the streets, dirty looking, smoking cigarettes, having fake tattoos, and risking their lives for a county charge (weenie offense) for seeking prostitution.

The county cop girls worked telephones, instead of the street, they holed up in fancy hotels near the airport, or even in prestigious downtown Clayton, Missouri. A certain type of weirdo desiring impersonal sex from a beautiful woman dialed a telephone number obtained from Backpage or gotten from another sexual deviant who can't seem to get enough. County cop girls answered their calls.

Sex talk led to names. Of course, both parties used an alias. One of the sex decoys was Detective Peggy. She was a gorgeous woman and still is. Very few men could resist Peggy.

There are buzz names floating around in the under-cover decoy sex trade circles. Powerful people with weaknesses tend to be big business. I don't mean business in terms of cash for the cop, but depending on the circumstances, a promotion may be in order somewhere down the line if a VIP is snagged in a sex sting. Some are politicians, business tycoons, wealthy people who inherited money, state prosecutors, people who are, the type of person who has enemies, political enemies.

Detective Peggy was working the phones and a mark called her. They sex talked and the guy was cooing on the other end of the line. "What's your name?" Peggy asked.

"Larry Johnson," the mark replied.

It was one of the buzz names the decoys had been ordered to watch for. Larry wasn't a guy who beat prostitutes or was obnoxious or dangerous in any way. He was just a sexual ghoul begging for gratification from a beautiful woman.

A meeting was set up at a hotel near the airport. It was a room with an adjoining room separated by a locked door. Peggy, as always, was looking good; she was fidgety and excited as she sat in the room, and a closed circuit television camera was recording her every move.

She had the appearance of a classy gal, one who had gone to private schools and lived in Ladue, or some other expensive neighborhood in west St. Louis County. But she was far from that. Peggy describes herself as a southside Hoosier; (not to be confused with the Hoosier who lives in Indiana) first police district, home of the South Broadway stroll where street hookers ply their trade.

That name, Hoosier, has been in St. Louis for centuries. It denotes poor working-class people, and neighborhoods. Hoosiers park their pickups in front of their houses, and sometimes on their lawns, or their neighbor's lawns. It is derogatory to anyone on the wrong end of any conversation. St. Louisans use it daily and everyone hates it. It only applies to white people, which is a breed becoming extinct in the City of St. Louis, Missouri.

White people, who for some stroke of luck, are financially able to afford a house in west St. Louis County, or even in St. Charles County, and take their lifestyle with them, are referred to as rich Hoosiers. The saying in those neighborhoods is, "There's no Hoosier like a rich Hoosier." Peggy was neither. She was just a gorgeous Hoosier gal from the southside. She had the ability to cut you just to watch you bleed. A trait most beautiful women are born with.

The tap on the door happened. Peggy glanced at the hidden surveillance camera, stood, and walked toward the door. She opened it and the usual conversation began; Larry Johnson strolled in, looking around the room, fearing for his safety, his security in life, his career, and marriage, but not so concerned that he decided to not risk it all for sexual gratification with a beautiful woman. Larry sat and stared at Detective Peggy; she was mesmerizing, friendly, smiling at him and engaging him.

Larry Johnson was the Circuit Attorney for the City of St. Louis, a political job to which he'd been reelected for years. He was a Democrat, but he had no choice, a Republican wouldn't be elected as dog catcher in the City of St. Louis.

Larry's problem, besides having an uncontrollable libido, was that he was a staunch conservative in a liberal city. The City of St. Louis, led and fed by its liberal newspaper, was dismantling before every citizen's eyes. It was and is a catastrophe in progress.

Larry wrote scathing letters to the editor which were printed in the dailies. He was one of the few citizens who wrote them on the side of conservatism. Nobody with an interest in their success in the city would take on city hall and the liberal newspaper.

But Larry was trusted and retained in the lead prosecutors' job often, and the stats concerning convictions were high. If Larry Johnson, Circuit Attorney for the City of St. Louis, took you to trial, you were as good as gone.

The stare-off continued, Peggy finally asked Larry Johnson the question: "What do you want?"

Larry stared and didn't immediately answer her. Here's where the irony, the shirtless fat man playing half-court in the summer heat comes in, reader friend. Larry Johnson was also a southside Hoosier. He and gorgeous Detective Peggy grew up in the same neighborhood. Larry was older, but somewhere down the line, he had seen her before, maybe walking in Carondelet Park, or in a grocery store with Peggy's parents. They had an invisible bond, which Larry took as a sexual bond, someone he could trust, a friend he could use for years to come. It was only money; sex was the important aspect of their possible long-range friendship.

Larry blurted out his sexual preference. The door to the adjoining room burst open and two undercover county cops rushed in, handcuffed Larry Johnson, and dragged him away.

Stellar police work by Detective Peggy. She would be awarded for her undercover prowess. Peggy was later promoted to sergeant.

That's the way it is in the cop/crook game. A winner and a loser. Was it because of the Larry Johnson arrest? The destruction of political enemy number one of the liberals and the newspaper in the city? Only the upper echelon of the political arena knows that answer.

Peggy married a county cop. He was a smart guy and he made rank, lots of rank. He was admired by his peers, married a gorgeous cop woman, and to top it off, he was a scratch golfer. They were a power couple within the department.

Peggy and hubs are retired now. Peggy sells real estate, hubs plays country club golf. He's the kind of guy who gets two holes in one during one round of golf. They mirror the lifestyles of the rich and famous.

9

BIG-BOB MEETS

RO-RO THE PO-PO

I had been involved in a serious auto accident on duty and was sequestered in the basement of headquarters answering telephones for a couple of years. Recovered, it was time to resume my cop duties. There were nine districts and three station houses.

The farthest south station house was referred to as south patrol. I had twenty-five years in the police department and had never been assigned south.

The first district, which I described in the previous chapter (Hoosier heaven) is where I was transferred. The captain, Tim Reagan, was a work friend. No anxiety.

I was assigned to the ten a.m. to six p.m. and six p.m. to two a.m. shift, twenty-one days of each shift. It was better than answering phones in the basement, and the predominantly white populace called the police for anything and everything. It was a busy district.

The new breed of gorgeous policewomen were there. I didn't wish to have a riding partner and I let that fact be known, so I rode alone in the winter darkness of south St. Louis, handling traffic accidents and peace disturbances, call after call. They never stopped.

Tim Reagan placed me on a prostitution detail, locking up the street hookers on South Broadway. Wallace Leopold was my partner. We had a lot of laughs together. Wallace was/is a smart guy, who graduated from Lynn University in Boca Raton, Florida.

He grew up in west St. Louis County; his dad had a business in Clayton, Missouri, the high-end part of the region. He had horses and drove Jaguars as a young adult and worked at his dad's store.

Boredom is a one-eyed monster. He tried to become a St. Louis County cop but they wouldn't hire him, so he paid his own way through the police academy, became certified by the State of

Missouri as a police officer, and was hired by the city. He is one of my closest friends.

The hooker detail petered out so Leopold and I went to different watches. I drew Big-Bob Weast as a riding partner. We rode in little Chevy cop cars with front-wheel drive. They were quick but fragile. Our shoulders touched as if we were attached, and when going around corners our bodies swayed in sync.

Big-Bob and I had great times together, and he also at this point in time is a close friend. There was a gorgeous girl on our watch, Rochelle, who referred to herself as Ro-Ro the Po-Po. She was big in stature, had large breasts, and had a huge personality. I rode with her occasionally. She would at times wear Bubba-Teeth as we rode around and she would smile and wave to the Hoosiers changing their oil in the street while their pickups were up on bumper jacks.

Cops get to know each other while they work. There are deep and personal conversations. Riding with someone for twenty-one days, especially when it's winter and dark gives each partner deep insight into their psyche.

The youngsters in the first district knew all about me. Intelligence Unit, DEA Task Force, Homicide, but now riding with them in a scout car. I had gotten in a fist fight with my Lieutenant and another cop, on duty, in the basement of headquarters. I figured the department was going to fire me, but that wasn't the case. That story, as well as dozens more, were told and retold by the young cops before I ever entered the south patrol station.

It didn't take long for Rochelle and I to become close friends. We liked each other and enjoyed our time together. We had laughs, just like I had done for most of my career, but I was concerned that Rochelle was getting too close and that she suspected we would be life-long friends; like I am with Big-Bob and Wally. It doesn't work that way with female partners. The male cop has a wife at home, in most cases. The female cop has or will have a boyfriend and husband eventually. The sexes don't allow closeness; unless the male cop is foolish.

The conversations continued; Ro told me about her past life. She had been a nanny for a drugged-out chiropractor in nearby Jefferson County, Missouri. The druggie had friends, and his friends as well as he, acted like one-percenter bikers. They dressed and acted the part, but were in real life, pussies.

This drugged employer of Ro, and his friends were into big-time bodybuilding. They used anabolic steroids, as well as cocaine. Ro dated one of the would-be bikers. He beat Ro with his fists and threw her down a flight of stairs that led to the sidewalk outside. She landed on the sidewalk.

The chiropractor decided to get clean and he entered rehab. Ro stayed on to nanny the two children. After the drying-out period, the chiropractor called and requested Ro pick him up at the rehab center and convey him home.

While driving the chiropractor home, she looked in the back seat where he had been sitting and observed him lying down in the seat, snorting cocaine. Ro became a car salesman and eventually was hired by the police department.

Big-Bob was divorced with two daughters. On the day watch, we would convey them to parochial school in the morning and pick them up in the afternoon. It was a tidy and solid way to wrap up my precarious cop career in Hoosier heaven.

Big-Bob and Rochelle began dating. It wasn't long before Rochelle became pregnant. She purchased a house on the southside on a cute little street where the houses are sitting on top of each other. It was small, but Big-Bob had carpentry skills and he was going to install a dormer and make a master bedroom.

Rochelle had a baby boy. While I was on duty, she asked me to come to her house and see her baby. It was winter and dark; I drove there in the police car. Big-Bob was there and he wasn't smiling. Rochelle asked me to hold the baby, so I reluctantly did. Holding babies isn't my forte, and I could tell that Ro was making long-range plans for Bob, and me, and she to be friends for life and that maybe someday the baby boy could refer to me as an uncle or something.

The scenario had train wreck written all over it. As I held the baby, Big-Bob was staring at me and then the baby, from several different angles. He was trying to see if I had anything to do with the kid. Ro was all bubbly and happy, and I asked her to take the baby. Bob was still staring.

I felt negative vibes in Ro's happy house. It was time to make an exit and I stood and walked to the door. Ro was standing, hugged me, Big-Bob stood and as I made it to the door, I could tell that Big-Bob wanted to leave with me. He was like a pet wanting to leave an unhappy home; hair of the dog.

It was obvious that Big-Bob didn't want to marry Ro-Ro the Po-Po. She was not reading the telltale signs. I felt bad for her. Big-Bob distanced himself from her, although he made his monthly child support payments. Ro was crushed. She was back to work and not happy. She looked to me for guidance but there was nothing I could do. This was so typical of cops and lifestyles that it caused embarrassment.

So, one evening Ro telephoned me at my residence; my wife was sitting next to me, and Ro was furious, screaming at me through the phone. Seems that she cornered Bob and asked him why he didn't want to marry her.

As usual, the third man out, a friend of both parties gets the blame; Bob told her that I told him that she got pregnant on purpose and that it totally turned him off. What girl doesn't get pregnant on purpose? It's why we're all here. I tried to calm Ro down, but the circumstances were too deep. I ended the conversation.

Ro was a thinker, and in her mind vengeance toward Big Bob was warranted. She sold her house, quit her cop job, absconded with the baby boy, and relocated to Mississippi. She got a cop job in a small town there, met, romanced, and wed an older fellow/cop. The old fellow legally adopted Big-Bob's son.

That meant that Big-Bob's kid was now his responsibility for the rest of his life, even if he and Ro divorced, which they did. Ro was tired of being a victim. It was her turn to be the victor.

Ro married a younger guy, a cop, and he had clout within the police department. Ro started making rank and climbed the ladder in the small department. She was sent to the prestigious F.B.I. National Academy in Quantico, Virginia.

But something happened in that small southern police department, a fight, or a disturbance; a fit of anger by a vengeful woman, but Ro-Ro the Po-Po was out of a job and out of another marriage.

Bits of information drifted back to the south city Hoosier police district. Big-Bob was beside himself wondering if he would ever see his only son again. He hasn't!

Big-Bob and I still talk. During a recent conversation, Ro-Ro the Po-Po came up. "You want to know what happened between me and Ro?" Bob asked.

Yeah," I replied.

"I met her dad," Bob said.

"What's that mean, Big-Bob?"

"Ro looks like her dad, spitting image. I couldn't get that out of my mind. I couldn't have sex with Ro anymore. I wanted to run, so I did. I didn't think I'd lose my son; I regret that."

10

POLICE WOMAN KATHY CENSKY;

TRUSTING, CARING; VICTIM

By the mid, to late 90s St. Louis policewomen were prevalent in every form of police life. They were supervisors, and detectives, rode horses in the mounted division and enjoyed the independence a job like St. Louis cop provided them.

The biweekly paycheck was always deposited into their bank account, with overtime. Vacations were scheduled, and if the cop could hang on long enough (20 years) a lifetime of retirement checks would be their reward.

Kathy Censky was a local girl who understood the excitement and diversity of being a St. Louis cop. She was single but dated. She was independent but devoted to her 4 horses and her mother, dad, and sister.

She worked to better herself; she was in great physical condition. She looked good in her mounted uniform while she rode her police horse. Whenever someone observed her on duty, riding, her great, hard body stood out. She was a sight to behold.

But, specialized jobs like mounted patrol don't last forever. If a new supervisor comes into a specialized unit, he/she desires to have his/her friends working for them. It isn't a civil service occupation. The job survives by smiles, intent, desires, and friends, within and without the police department. No position is secure. If you love your specialized assignment you are going to get your heart broken.

Kathy rode in mounted for several years, and then was booted back to district patrol duties. In reality, there are no bad jobs within the police department, unless the cop gets assigned to prisoner processing, booking prisoners, and checking cells full of weirdos.

Kathy was assigned to the third police district (south city) and quickly fell back into the life of a district cop, show up for work, answer your radio, write a few moving traffic violations, a few parking tags, and if you are lucky, go home at the end of your shift.

The district cop, in most cases, doesn't have to deal with long-drawn-out court procedures or working informants in the ever-present search for criminal information (life of a detective) or striving to make a name for oneself to impress a supervisor (few can be impressed). Their job, in actuality, is to stay alive, uninjured and radio responsive.

It's a simple life, and there is downtime.

Cops are required to write their police reports in the field. Seven-Eleven Convenience Stores had offices for cops, with telephones and desks. Cops were prevalent in those stores, and the area cop became acquainted with the employees and the customers.

Kathy was outgoing, she loved people and animals. She became friendly with a local motorcycle club, The Statesmen. The Statesmen MC was a south St. Louis group of Harley riders. They had a clubhouse, wore colors, and were close-knit. They weren't an outlaw biker group, but they wanted to be, so they acted the part, had tough guys as members, and took long rides as a group. Kathy was impressed.

People like Kathy are easily taken advantage of. They deeply feel that if they like a person or group, then that person or group will like them. What the casual observer doesn't realize is that most of the guys and gals in a wannabe outlaw motorcycle group have a deep hatred for cops or any kind of authority. It's why they desire to belong to a group of nonconforming subculture outlaws.

Kathy saw the surface of the Harley riders. What she didn't see was the lifestyle of the biker gangs. If, when a member of an outlaw biker gang is arrested, brought into a district station in handcuffs, and placed in a chair amongst cops, they are at first verbally abused, for the cops hate the bikers as much as the bikers hate authority. The bikers talk back to the cops, answering a question with a question. It goes downhill from there.

In some instances, the bikers are physically abused, slapped, body punched, humiliated, and beaten with telephone books. When the cuffs click on every cop is a badass. Many aren't in a one-on-one fight.

Kathy became friends with The Statesmen MC. She purchased a used Harley Davidson motorcycle and she was learning how to ride it. Her immediate supervisor caught wind that Kathy was hanging out with police characters. The Statesmen MC were considered outlaws by cops. They didn't have one-percenter status like the Hells Angels or The Banditos, but they desired it; at least they did twenty years ago when this incident occurred. Word on the street was that they were trying to get a Hells Angels charter, and Kathy advised her sister, Debbie Jenicek, that they were trying to get/become Hells Angels charter status.

The Statesmen MC was having a party on The Landing, a nightclub district in downtown St. Louis by the Mississippi River, just north of The Gateway Arch. Kathy invited her sister to the event.

Her sister, (Debbie) was shocked at The Statesmen MC. It was a motorcycle gang and her little sister was a part of it, and she was a City of St. Louis cop. Debbie asked Kathy to get away and to stay from The Statesmen MC.

Kathy replied, "Don't worry about it, I'll be okay." Debbie understood Kathy; she knew Kathy was constantly seeking thrills; it was Kathy's nature.

Debbie left The Landing deeply concerned for Kathy's safety. She couldn't figure out or understand why Kathy wanted to associate with them, thrills notwithstanding.

Kathy continued her association with The Statesmen MC. They had planned a ride to Kentucky Lake. Some of the group would ride their Harley's to the lake; some would have them conveyed in an enclosed trailer. Kathy's Harley was conveyed.

The bikes were unloaded and the ride around Kentucky Lake proceeded. Kathy was riding beside one of The Statesmen. It should be noted that Kathy was an equine barrel racer. She could handle herself while straddling a horse or a Harley.

The riders were traveling East on Highway 62 approaching Highway 641 beside the lake. A Statesmen member told the Marshall County Deputy Sheriff that Kathy apparently lost control of the Harley as she rounded a curve in the road and traveled into the median strip; she continued East across Highway 641 and struck a curb. The Harley jumped the curve and traveled alongside the road on a descending rock/riprap embankment and Kathy was thrown off of the Harley. Kathy apparently went straight instead of taking the curve.

Someone went for help or to find a telephone to call the Sheriff and an ambulance. Kathy lay on the rocks beside the lake semi-conscious, in deep shock. She had a broken neck. Someone in the group of The Statesmen decided to fleece Kathy of her wallet, pistol, badge, and identification identifying her as a City of St. Louis Police Officer, and any cash she had on her. They didn't steal her jewelry though, commendable.

When the Deputy Sheriff and the ambulance arrived (no telling how long that took) Kathy had a weak heartbeat. The deputy took statements from several witnesses at the scene. Only one witness was associated with The Statesmen MC, a female. The other witnesses only observed Kathy going toward the rocks along the side of the road.

The female Statesmen MC associate stated in the official incident report that she was riding next to Kathy Censky when Kathy lost control of her Harley, jumped the curb, and went into the riprap.

I interviewed another witness to the incident, from Calvert City, Ky. He advised me that he didn't see the entire accident, but he observed Kathy Censky next to a male rider and that Kathy's attention was for some reason directed toward the beach area of the lake; she didn't make the curve, she jumped the curb and headed into the riprap.

The male witness stated that he observed four or five motorcycle riders at the scene. He also advised me that he has never been contacted by any police organization concerning the accident. I asked him if he knew that Kathy Censky was an active St. Louis police officer. He stated, "yes!"

It seemed odd to me that the male witness would know about Kathy's cop job. Only the Statesmen MC members at the scene had that information. It was also odd that he advised me that he observed Kathy riding next to a male, not a female. The female MC associate stated that she was riding next to Kathy.

The two other witnesses were not members of the group. They were apparently drivers passing by. But it should be noted that I attempted to identify them and contact them for an interview and there is no evidence of them ever existing. The Kentucky Lake ride was apparently a big deal for The Statesmen MC. I wondered why no other club members were listed as witnesses; maybe the larger group continued to ride leaving the one female to talk to the first responders. A slight bump by a rider could have sent Kathy reeling and losing control. Apparently, speed was a factor.

The deputy obtained Kathy's name from the female Statesmen and a possible next of kin and telephone number (her sister) in south St. Louis County. There was no mention of Kathy being an active member of the St. Louis Metropolitan Police Department.

Kathy was conveyed to Benton, KY, and eventually died in the Benton Hospital emergency room. The coroner was also the emergency room doctor on duty when Kathy was brought into the ER. He telephoned Kathy's sister Debbie Jenicek and informed her of her sister's death. The coroner/doctor advised Debbie that he tried to save Kathy but couldn't. The coroner asked Debbie if she could give some identifying features of Kathy.

Debbie advised the coroner that Kathy had a tattoo of a butterfly on her right hip. A tattoo of a bull's head skull with horns on her right buttocks, and breast implants. Debbie asked the coroner why he needed verification of Kathy's tattoos; she asked him where her Police Department Identification and badge were and her pistol.

The coroner was shocked. He told Debbie that no one knew Kathy was a police officer, and that there were no credentials with the body. By then, the Statesmen MC was headed back to St. Louis.

Kathy had several abrasions; one on the center of her forehead. An abrasion extending the length of her nose. Two small abrasions on her left arm, one at the side of her wrist and another one at the armpit. An abrasion going around her chin and a large laceration on the posterior cranial portion of her head. X-rays revealed Kathy had fractures of the 1st and 2nd cervical vertebra which caused her death.

She also had a fracture to the left scapula and a fracture of the pelvis.

The death occurred on May 23, 1998, at approximately 2:00 p.m. She was pronounced at 3:32 p.m. Kathy was 42 years of age. Debbie Jenicek, after being advised by the Benton Kentucky Coroner that Kathy didn't have her credentials or her pistol, responded to Kathy's house. There was a lock box installed on a wall in her house specifically for her pistol and credentials. Debbie checked it, it was unlocked and empty. Her driver's license and badge turned up later in Kentucky, but not her pistol.

The mystery of the missing pistol continued. As family members were moving items from Kathy's house, the pistol was found in the oven of the kitchen stove. Debbie is certain that Kathy didn't put it there. She never left her house without it. Whoever took it returned the pistol to Kathy's house and hid it in the oven to be found by whomever.

It doesn't appear that there was any further investigation into Kathy's demise. Her death was not investigated by the St. Louis Metropolitan Police Department; it wasn't their crime; it was Marshall County, Kentucky's crime if indeed there was a crime.

I was dispatched to Kathy's house on Alaska the evening of her death. A high-ranking police officer showed up and we checked the exterior of the house. There was no forced entry. I asked him what was going on. He said, "they killed her."

A cop friend recently advised me that Kathy was intoxicated at the time of her death. I asked him how he knew that. He said that was the cop rumor.

As far as the city cops were concerned, Kathy was advised to stay away from The Statesmen MC. She didn't heed the warnings of her supervisors. When that happens the upper echelon cops turn their backs on the cop/victim, dead or alive. They obviously turned their backs on Police Officer Kathy Censky.

There was a large attendance at Kathy's wake. Most of The Statesmen MC members showed up. They came in casually dressed and then asked Kathy's mother if they could don their "colors" and come back inside. She advised them it was okay. They exited, and then returned with their MC colors on.

At the funeral, there was a large procession. The Statesmen MC rode their Harley's to the cemetery. Debbie recognized two City of St. Louis Police Officers who were friends with Kathy, Jimmy Moran, and Joe Richardson.

Debbie observed two other people casually dressed in blazers who didn't join in with the crowd but stayed back and observed. One of them had a pistol in a holster. She asked Joe Richardson and Jimmy Moran who they were. Jimmy and Joe didn't know them.

City cops? Marshall County, Kentucky cops? Doubtful. Alcohol Tobacco and Firearms (ATF) agents, probably.

The incident was at the very least a suspicious death; at the very most, a homicide. It should have been investigated. It wasn't! There is no statute of limitation on murder. Kathy's demise is super cold; cold cases get solved daily.

I decided to probe into this cold case, the possible homicide of a City of St. Louis female Police Officer. I telephoned the female MC associate who had given the statement to the Kentucky Deputy first responder, who was listed in the incident report as the female who was riding next to Kathy.

The female associate was friendly and convincing as she described to me what had transpired on that sunny day at Kentucky Lake. Her husband is a member of the Statesmen MC; females are not allowed to be members.

She stated that they had just started their ride and Kathy Censky was riding next to her. They were both thrilled to be riding on this perfect day and they were riding slowly, just about 25 MPH when for some unknown reason Kathy's motorcycle veered in front of her bike. She said that Kathy was smiling at her and that Kathy lost control of the Harley; it went over a curb and into the riprap leading down toward the beach and the water. Kathy was thrown off and landed on the riprap.

I asked about the first responders and the fact that they didn't know Kathy was an active police officer, or that Kathy's gun and badge or credentials were not with her when she was transported to the hospital. She didn't comment on the question.

When conducting a telephone interview there is only so much information the interviewer can get. He/she isn't in the position to challenge the person being interviewed, just ask the questions and try to get a response. The content is then deciphered by the interviewer after the call.

She unwittingly gave me information. I didn't advise her that the other witness, had advised me that he observed Kathy riding next to a male rider, not a female.

The associate, witness advised me that Kathy was having a fling with one of the male members; "she liked him much more than he liked her," she continued.

"What was his name," I asked.

"Roller is his club name, I'd have to look up his real name," she replied.

The female witness and I small talked about her life for the past twenty years since the incident with Kathy Censky. She's led a hard-working life.

I felt empty after interviewing her. Her story and the details didn't pan out for me. The male witness interview was 180 degrees from hers. For one, at the speed the female witness said they were going at 25 MPH Kathy would have been able to stop her Harley. The injuries sustained by Kathy were indicative of a high-speed motorcycle crash.

The statement by her that she didn't know the name of the club member romantically involved with Kathy; she said "Roller". The inconsistencies are boundless.

I contacted Debbie Jenicek, Kathy's sister, and advised her of the interview. Debbie advised me that Kathy was romantically involved with a member called, "Enforcer".

I asked Debbie how she knew that; she said that after Kathy's death she was contacted by the guy, Enforcer, who stated he had some items in Kathy's house that he wanted to retrieve, a gun and some night vision binoculars.

Debbie advised that she met Enforcer at Kathy's house and gave him the items he requested. Debbie said he was a scary guy with mean eyes.

Debbie Jenicek advised me that the female witness/associate of the Statesman MC is a liar and that she sought Debbie out at Kathy's wake and went into bizarre details about the incident. Debbie felt she was lying to her.

After pondering the telephone interview and investigating the comments made by the female witness/Statesman MC associate, I determined that she lied to me four times.

There is a jurisdictional problem with the case; it happened in Kentucky, and this retired cop, who isn't a cop anymore, resides in in St. Louis County, Missouri.

So, my reader friend, was this the perfect crime, a murder of a wayward policewoman, a thrill seeker who couldn't satisfy her desires wearing a badge and the blue uniform on the nasty streets of the City of St. Louis?

Maybe!

11

DAWN

BUBBLES-SURFER-GIRL

Dawn Huckfeldt was/is a blonde and blue, cute energetic outgoing young woman. Her main nickname is Bubbles. She grew up in St. Louis and, like most of the inhabitants of the region, knew and respected St. Louis cops. City cops were heroes in those golden days of law enforcement. The city was full of monsters; the cops were their slayers.

She took the cop entrance test in the late-90s and was accepted. After the police academy, she was sent to the fourth police district (downtown St. Louis) the best district to work in; and continued with her unstoppable energy.

Dawn worked in the projects for three years, a daunting task. Her supervisor Was Sergeant Bob Berner, a good guy, cop, and boss. Bob was transferred to the bikes/beats, and Dawn was eventually placed into the fourth district bikes/beats. It's how it works in big-city police departments.

Bike/beats has to be the best job in the city. The cops (including me) rode 21-speed Trek Mountain Bikes around the downtown area, answering calls and having fun. Even in the winter, the job was fun.

We basically chose our own partners; Dawn chose Officer Brian Min as hers. Brian (Asian) former Marine, as energetic as Dawn, and a great cop (he could have been a character actor in Hollywood) worked well together.

Brian came from the bloody third district; he had another female cop partner, Angela Luong. They were making a drug arrest at a house of interest when one of the people hanging around the drug den took off running. Brian gave chase into an alleyway. Brian caught the runner and they scuffled. The guy tried to wrestle Brian's gun away from him and Brian shot him. It was a clear case of self-defense. Angela eventually quit the police department; Brian was transferred to fourth district bikes/beats.

Brian and Dawn were a sight to behold riding their bicycles downtown. The smooth Asian and the blonde surfer girl, her ponytail bobbing up and down as she sped along.

Brian was a prankster; he would target other cops and prank them regularly. He was also a voice imitator. He could imitate any voice, and on the telephone, the caller never knew he was talking to an impostor. He targeted supervisors.

Dawn married Rick Feldman, a guy old enough to be her dad. His dad, Ray Feldman, owned Ray's Auto Parts on Dr. Martin Luther King. Steve Waldman (first chapter) worked at the store. Both Rick, Steve, and Ray knew boatloads of city cops. Cops are always looking for a place to hang out; Ray's was the place.

Rick was into motorcycles, and he purchased himself and Dawn Harley Davidson Motorcycles, Springer models, top of the line. He (like all guys) envisioned himself riding with Dawn, the cute surfer girl cop that he owned because he was a stud, in his mind, and she could get him out of speeding tickets.

They weren't married long and Dawn met a Hispanic city cop and became infatuated with him. She divorced Rick Feldman. He promptly reclaimed his property (Harley) which was in Rick's name.

Ray, Rick's dad, mostly sold automobile paint to body shops. He had a contract with Dupont, and his prices were usually better than the other paint stores. He sold a lot of paint.

The problem with automobile paint is that when it gets old it's expensive to dispose of. Ray had a couple of guys working for him, doing odd jobs, and Ray advised them to take the old paint and convey it to a disposal company in East St. Louis.

The workers loaded some barrels of paint onto an old pickup truck and drove to the St. Louis Riverfront. They dumped the paint into the Mississippi River. The Environmental Protection Agency doesn't think highly of things being dumped into the Mississippi River. They arrested the guys.

They said they were just doing what they were told by Ray Feldman. The feds believed them, arrested Ray and Ray ultimately went to prison. So, Rick was out of a cute young blonde wife and Ray was on his way to federal incarceration. The business stayed open, barely, because everybody liked Ray, not Rick. But Rick had two Harley's.

Dawn and her Hispanic cop were hot and heavy. They camped together, drank together, and partied together, until one evening, for an unknown reason, the cop beat Dawn up with his fists.

Dawn was shocked. She didn't go to the ER, but her face was swollen and her lip was split; she was ashamed that her cop boyfriend pummeled her. But she did go to the police department's Internal Affairs Division and made a formal complaint. Nothing was ever done.

The Hispanic cop eventually was involved in another fight off-duty and quit before he could be fired. Dawn dated around, nothing serious, and eventually met and married another city cop. They had a daughter. She still bopped around downtown with her ponytail flying; she had the smallest child's bike Trek bikes made.

In the fall of 2004, the Baseball Cardinals were involved in some playoff games. The ball team and their stadium is sacred ground for St. Louis Police, as important as the brewery, Budweiser, Michelob Ultra, and Busch Barbarian Beer.

The fourth District Captain was Mary Warnecke; she needed to cover herself in case someone is robbed at or near the stadium. If there was a street robbery on those sacred lands, the bosses in the Ivory Tower would be asking her what she did to prevent it. She assigned Dawn, and another newer hard-charging cop, Matt Browning, to work undercover in and around the stadium primarily looking for robbers who strongarm people for their tickets.

Matt was intense to the extent of scary. The cop job actually isn't like that; it's fun most of the time. It has its own intensity and there is no need to add to that. Matt didn't understand the job. He sat, brooded, and smoked cigarettes like a Hollywood detective trying to solve a heinous murder.

He was a city kid; his dad was a retired fireman, and no doubt somewhere down the line there's a friend politician who told Matt to work hard and he'd get him promoted to sergeant, the rank most of the cops are striving for, (except for me). Matt wasn't physical, didn't work out or try to better himself. His political ties ruined him.

Dawn and Matt, in civilian clothing, were given a small economy undercover car, a Dodge Neon, to patrol with. They circled the stadium scanning the crowds looking for suspected street robbers, or anyone approaching sports fans going to the game.

There were other detectives patrolling, and one of the crews arrested two people for allegedly trying to boost tickets from an elderly couple. They were in a conveyance vehicle (paddy wagon) for transport to the area station to be booked and processed.

One of the arrestees was a female, and in those cases, a female cop is required to respond to the scene of the arrest to search them for weapons or contraband. The area sergeant responded to the scene of the arrest and two additional detectives responded. Their cars were lined up behind the paddy wagon partially in the street.

Dawn and Matt responded and parked their Neon in the line of cars. The rear doors of the paddy wagon were open and the two of them walked up to the open doors where several cops and detectives were standing. The suspects were inside with handcuffs on.

Dawn climbed inside and did a cursory search of the female arrestee. Matt stood at the rear of the van and began interrogating them. It wasn't his arrest and he had no purpose there, but he was unrelenting. He wanted to write a memorandum to Captain Mary Warnecke to show how dedicated he was. It was overkill and embarrassing to veteran cops.

His interrogation was so juvenile that when Dawn had the suspect remove her shoes, somehow one of the shoes was thrown at Matt, maybe by a cop. The area supervisor kept saying, "Get him out of here," to Dawn, but she was inside the van not really knowing where Matt was coming from. He was her partner for the night and she was loyal to their partnership.

Dawn had some kind of attachment to Matt, maybe because in her whole life Matt was someone who was as miserable as she. Even though she doesn't know why, she remained loyal to him to the end.

The end came quickly; a ballgame cretin driving with a blood alcohol content three times over the limit crashed into the line of cars behind the paddy wagon. It sent the line of cars toward the paddy wagon trapping Matt and severing his legs. It's a tough job, reader friends.

The seasoned cops calmly called for EMS for an officer down while they scrambled to back the cars up to get the car off of Matt's gone legs. Dawn freaked when she realized what had happened. She tried to help Matt and stop the bleeding while waiting for EMS to arrive. Someone arrested the drunk driver. EMS arrived and transported Matt. Both legs were gone; he was in his mid-twenties.

Friends, relatives, and people interested in cops, tried to counsel Matt. There's a worker's compensation clause that states the disabled worker can get a disability pension or a worker's compensation lump sum, but not both. Matt had to decide which he wanted to take. He was still being paid by the police department, and he could have continued in the department in a clerical job, but there's another clause that states each officer must complete and pass the physical agility test. Obviously, Matt could not.

During Matt's rehabilitation Dawn was at his beck and call. She visited him regularly at the hospital and did his bidding. She was using her family time to tend to Matt. Her husband wanted to know why. Her daughter was being cared for by the in-laws; Dawn devoted all of her free time to Matt.

Dawn's supervisors noted her behavior and took her off of the street. She was transferred to an evidence unit (CSI) and processed crime scenes. She was/is smart, and motivated, and she took to it with enthusiasm, like she does everything.

The already shaky cop marriage became shakier. It eventually dissolved, one of the cop curses, divorce, alcohol, debt, PTSD. Dawn was suffering from PTSD but didn't realize it. After this divorce, she took up with another man, a guy from southern California.

He wanted to go back there; he did and Dawn quit her cop job and followed him. She had twelve years in the police department. She got a job working for a company that investigates cash flow between institutions and individuals, and she applied for the Orange County Sheriff's Department.

She was hired and was preparing to go into the police academy when the relationship crashed. Nothing new for Dawn. She knew in her heart that the St. Louis Metropolitan Police Department would hire her again.

She had been away from her daughter and missed her. She came back to the police department but they refused to rehire her, reason unknown to Dawn, but peculiar behavior is duly noted and used against cops.

She applied for a job at the brewery and was hired as a bottler, which pays more than being a St. Louis cop. She purchased a house in Jefferson County Missouri, and regained custody of her daughter.

She is still suffering from PTSD and is on disability leave from the brewery. She's still loyal to Matt Browning, visiting and counseling him, spending valuable time with him. Misery loves company.

Matt never did progress into prosthetics. Athletic people strive for the freedom of using artificial limbs; the police department would have paid for them, but Matt isn't athletic. He uses a wheelchair.

He ran for Alderman of his southside neighborhood. He asked for the backing of the St. Louis Police Officers Association (cop union). He didn't get it. He lost.

Dawn was recently laid-off from her brewery job.

12

THE TWO CHRISTY'S & THE RED BOMBER

The young talented female cops were ensconced in the south patrol station house. The captains of the first, second, fourth, and ninth districts showed great interest in some of them. They would not be sent to any of the other districts; those were black districts. A call would be made to the personnel division to see how the gals tested on the entrance exam.

The ones who tested high were targeted for mentoring. They were coddled, given a good riding partner, and not required to work any details; unless there was some sort of glory attached to them.

There was a change in the cop/crook game. Knuckle draggers, night stick-wielding burly cops, bad attitude beer guzzlers were not appreciated in the business anymore. They were tolerated but not given any credence. The department desired intellectual applicants and members.

These gals who came into the job were there because they desired to be. It wasn't just a job that one could do for twenty or thirty years and receive a pension. They came educated, intelligent and pro-company. In any corporation, employers always look for the best and the brightest; the police department is no different.

Christy Long was a long-legged blonde, smart and cute, but one of her most revered traits was that she was cunning. That plays big in the cop/crook game. Christy and I were on the same watch although we never rode together. She had a partner who drove her around, protected her, and allowed her to be relaxed in the passenger seat while he drove.

The South Broadway stroll was in full bloom with prostitutes. Christy was put out on the street walking and waving at cars. She didn't snag any customers for several days. She tried to look the part, dressed down, dirty looking, and she had the body that the Johns were looking for, but they shied away from her.

So, Christy started acting; she was a good actress; she played the part of a heroin junky going through withdrawal, looking sick, chain-smoking cigarettes, and quickly walking up and down South Broadway.

It worked and she nabbed a few horny old men. Captain Tim Reagan took her off of the detail. It was just something to pad her resume. It was common knowledge that if and when she took the promotional test to sergeant, she'd ace it. She was that smart.

In contrast, was Christy M. She was small, almost too small for the game. She tried to hide in her uniform. It hung on her; like it was a couple of sizes too large, and she always wore her cop hat. She was a friendly gal if and when she would acknowledge you, but she was always watching and assessing and searching for a way to survive in the nasty game of cops and robbers.

Before I rode with Ro-Ro, Christy wanted us to be partners. I begged off, and told her he didn't wish to ride with a female, which was in part truth, but not wholly true.

I knew Christy was married, had a daughter, and lived in the district. Her husband was a City of St. Louis Fireman. Between the two salaries they were doing okay, but I sensed all was not well in the marriage. Cops, firemen, and old seasoned detective tossed back into the district life; it had disaster written all over it, and besides, Christy was so small she could no way protect herself against a man. Which meant I would be doing all of the fighting. I had had that experience in law enforcement and didn't wish to go back to it.

Christy M's dad was the Chief of Police of another City of St. Louis Police Department, which explained how she got hired, and why she was in South Patrol. Christy, while I was riding with Ro-Ro, approached me. "Why would you ride with her but not with me?" she defiantly asked.

"I don't make the worksheets, Christy," I replied.

So eventually, after Ro-Ro absconded with Big-Bob's kid, I found myself riding around in the dark with little Christy M. As usual, the life stories poured out. She and the hubs were not doing well, blah, blah, blah. Seems that Christy liked to go to the nightspots in the eastside, all night, while hubs was snoozing at the firehouse, and the hubs couldn't understand this practice. God only knows how my name was tossed around.

So, one day on the day watch, I received a radio call for a 911 hang-up, which means that someone took the time and effort to dial 911, and then decided not to speak to the dispatcher.

I had never been to Christy's house but I drove to the address and knocked on the door. Things were quiet, so I tried the door and it was unlocked; I pushed it open and looked inside. Christie and the hubs were inside, standing; hubs had his hand behind his back, which in cop survival 101 means there's likely a weapon in the hidden hand. Christy looked disheveled.

They didn't expect me to come by their house and push their door open, and I didn't expect to see them standing and obviously fighting when I pushed open the door, so it was a standoff and the three of us stared. Finally, I said, "Everything okay here, Christy?"

"Yes," she replied. The fireman glared at me with hatred. I figured in his mind he suspected that I was partying with his little wife on the eastside while he was snoozing at the firehouse. Untrue and a dangerous scenario. Jealously gets people killed daily.

I nodded and backed off, got into the police car, and responded to other calls. The next day Christy was at the station; I asked her what was going on. "We were fighting and he had a gun, he said he was going to shoot me, I tried to dial 911 and he grabbed the phone before I could talk to the dispatcher. We saw you drive up. He told me to be still and that if you came into the house, he was going to kill you and me. That's when you pushed the door open. I did everything I could to keep you from coming inside. He would have shot you."

"That's nice, Christy," I sarcastically replied.

Christy eventually divorced, quit the police department, and went to Philadelphia to be a cop. Her mother and her sisters lived there.

Back to Christy Long:

Christy was promoted to sergeant and sent to the central patrol division. The commander of the ninth district was Captain Larry O'Toole. The mentoring of Christly Long continued.

Larry was a divorced cop. The strange thing about cops was that most were divorced. It seemed like the job took priority in their lives; marriage came second. Most women don't accept being second best.

The other strange phenomenon is that when we (cops) retire, the ex-wife gets a percentage of our pension. Sometimes fifty percent. Cops languish in their promotions. It's billed as the common denominator between success and failure. It means, "I'm better than you."

In a quasi-military operation like police work, the commander of a district is all-seeing, doing, being, or thinks he/she is, and if a subordinate would question the authority of the commander he is banished from any/all promotions.

I worked for Larry O'Toole. He had five years in the police department and was already a supervisor (sergeant). I had twenty years as a cop and was his underling.

Larry had ambitions and drive, and influential relatives. Mentoring a luscious blonde female cop was right in his wheelhouse. Larry O'Toole treated me well.

Christy met and started dating Mike Marks, who had just been promoted to sergeant. Mike had been married a couple of times and he was a young guy. Christy would give Larry O'Toole a play-by-play of her and Mike Marks's relationship. It was allegedly part of the mentoring process. Mike didn't know the mentoring went into their personal lives. I was work friends with the three of them.

To keep dedication in perspective, my reader friend, Mike Marks was/is a sharp guy. He could have done anything in life he desired. His family had a plumbing company in south St. Louis. He was a master journeyman plumber by trade. He grew up in south St. Louis, so he knew the lay of the land. He trained physically at a neighborhood gym where cops trained. He listened to their stories, mimicked them, and desired to be them.

In contrast, reader friend, I went into the Marine Corps at the age of seventeen. The only contact I had with cops was when I was getting speeding tickets. I didn't expect or desire to be a cop, but life happens. The St. Louis Police Department was hiring cops. The Marine Corps experience made me qualified.

Guys like Mike Marks, gals like Christy Long, they came here to succeed. Making rank was and is the criteria for success, as previously stated. I became a cop so I could drive fast, drink beer, and beat people up. But the police department tricked me. They made a free University of Missouri education available to me. So, the worm turned and I became a semi-company man for as long as it was beneficial to me. Mike and Christy and Larry lived their sordid lives on closed-circuit police department television (regrettably we all did). Everyone commented, laughed, and shook their heads in disbelief. There are no secrets in the cop job. Everyone is related to you and everyone knows your personal business.

Continuing with perspective, reader friend; I was a field training officer for a young intelligent woman, Renee Kriesmann. We got along well and had fun on the cop job. After we settled into our routine together she asked me, "why does your wife hate you?"

I never mentioned my wife or my family to her. I was twice her age and had been a cop for twenty years. I blew the question off. My marital problems were in the past. But it reinforced my understanding of the cop job; everybody knows everything about everyone.

Renee made rank; she's a major now and could quite possibly be the next chief of police. She's serious and dedicated and an administrator. She impresses people outside of the police department who are in powerful positions.

I retired from the cop job, but Mike Marks and his stories filtered down to me. Mike eventually married Christy. They had two children and lived in Mike's house (which was in his mom's name). Christy was promoted to Lieutenant and Larry O'Toole was promoted to Major. The mentoring continued.

The rumors zipped through the police department like sniper fire. People would tell Christy that Mike was dating other women. Mike would get rumors that Christy and Larry O'Toole were playing games.

Cops don't come home on some nights. It's usually the job, or the second job, or overtime. But distrust festers like a foot wound. They split; Christy's parents purchased a house for her in south county (not the Island) and then the divorce happened.

It was a big trial and it lasted four days. They called witnesses, and Mike Marks subpoenaed Larry O'Toole. On the stand, Mike's attorney asked Larry if he had ever had sex with Christy. He said, "no!"

Larry was asked if he had ever been to Christy's house in south county in the evening   He said, "yes!"

Christy took the stand and said that Mike beat her, raped her continuously, and was unfaithful to her. The show went on and on and nobody won. It was just another cop show for the minions of the police department to dwell on for a day or two and then it would be on to another disaster.

Mike is still a Sergeant. Christy is now a Captain. Larry O'Toole is a retired Lieutenant Colonel, who was trying to be the Chief of Police right up to the moment of his retirement.

The Red Bomber: Katie Mandel was/is a gorgeous gal. Any man who meets her becomes infatuated with her. She graduated from nursing school while still a teenager, worked in the trade for several years, and then decided she wanted to be a St. Louis cop.

She dated another young cop, dedicated and serious about a job that neither was warranted during the 50s, 60s, or 70s, (good old boys club rules) but became crucial as the decades clicked by.

Katie was super cool as well as gorgeous and smart. I never worked with her but had had training with her, and lunch with her on a couple of occasions. There were some stares of desire between the two of us, but nothing more.

She had a couple of kids and, as in most of the cop marriages, suspected her hubs was seeing other women (she told me that) so Katie took the kids and left for higher ground. They ultimately divorced.

Katie bounced around the country working in hospitals as an RN. Her children are grown. She was living and nursing in San Diego as of last year. She married a guy who's a cop somewhere in California.

Her dream is to relocate to a third-world country and live the good life with a cop she recently married.

Steve Waldman

Kathy Censky. Loved the excitement of the job. Paid for her professionally taken photo of her in her uniform

Attorney John Haugh, Pipefitters Local 562 Workers
Compensation Attorney. Murdered in Miami. Not
solved.

Joann Lipscomb. Brutally murdered on duty by a city of St. Louis police officer's son.

Dawn, Bubbles, Surfer girl. Fighting PTSD and winning.

Christy Marks and the author. An old friend from
South Patrol. Smart, made rank, married a city cop,
Mike Marks. I'm friends with both of them.

Detective Sergeant Andria
VanMierlo, St. Louis County,
retired.

Isabella Lovadina. Hero cop. Involved in an off-duty incident; her heroic response saved lives; shot critically; she never gave up and fought with the attackers to the end.

City cop, Brian Min. Great cop, a funny guy. Dawn
(Bubbles, Surfer girl's partner in the Bikes and Beats).

Mike Braun, my partner at DEA. Became the Director of Operations at the federal agency. Now working in the private sector.

Author and Aggie Santangelo, retired city police detective. She now owns and operates Café Dolce on The Hill in south St. Louis. Best coffee house in the region.

Big Bob Weast; close friend, old riding partner in the south patrol.

Lieutenant Alana Hauck (right) with her wife.

Katie Mandel, city cop and R/N. Married a city cop, had two kids, divorced, and left St. Louis to resume her career in nursing.

LeAnn Robertson. St. Louis County Police Officer for several years. Resigned and went to an outstate police department. Critically injured by a handcuffed suspect, and then was critically injured in an auto accident while on duty.

Kaitlin Alix, stunning beauty, killed by a fellow officer playing with guns.

Police Officer Trent Koppel, Des Peres, Missouri police officer. Award-winning investigator, now in corporate security.

Intelligence Unit Detective Patty Rice. Medal of Valor Winner.

Sergeant Dave Bonenberger. Hero cop, smart, talented guy, Daph's husband.

Bailey Coletta, lied to the FBI and a federal grand jury; she felt compelled to lie to protect her boyfriend. The feds know the answers to the questions before they ask them. Her boyfriend went to prison for a long time. She got a light sentence and she lost her cop job.

Sergeant Jeff Kowalski. Shot in the gut, took him
twenty years to die. Married to Kimberly Kowalski at
the time of his death.

Kathy Censky's Harley; her pride and joy. She died
while riding it.

Jenna Diehl Christian, left. Critically injured in an on-duty car pursuit.

Liz Baker, in survival mode.

Kim Kowalski, cute, smart, spunky, determined. Left alone to raise her children. Attends every parole hearing of the street criminal who murdered her husband.

Jan Fore, Naïve, vulnerable, nice person.

Captain David Dorn with his wife, Sergeant Ann Dorn.

13

ISABELLA LOVADINA

THE BRAVEST COP

Isabella, "God is my oath" was one of the "new" female recruits hitting the streets of the nasty town of St. Louis, Missouri. She was/is cute, single, and adventurous.

She wanted a job where she could make a difference; she wanted to contribute to her city and country. It is a good job, fun at first, trying as the years speed by. She wasn't looking for a man friend, she didn't go to singles bars, she worked and took courses to better herself in her profession.

She met a City of St. Louis Fire Fighter, Nick Koenig, on a call for a traffic accident. They became friends, were taking the same EMS course, and studied together. It was a relationship, but not hot and heavy.

Nick was a city kid and his relatives lived in the city. His grandmother lived at 902 Hickory, just off of the interstate and close to the Gateway Arch in a rehabbed area of the city. Old brick houses are rejuvenated in the City of St. Louis, they have value and character.

Nick invited Isabella to the house for dinner and to study, and at about 0030 in the winter of 2009, Nick walked Isabella out to her car. They stood next to the car, and Isabella placed her gun and vest inside the car.

A car pulled up with screeching tires and two males jumped out, both armed with handguns. "Give us your money," they demanded. Neither Nick nor Isabella had any money on them. Street robber's figure if the victim is white, they've got money.

The robbers threatened to kill them, and then one of them said, "who's in the house?"

"There's women and children in the house," Nick said.

The robbers forced them into the house and ordered them to kneel on the floor in the hallway. They continued to threaten them with their guns, telling them they were going to kill them. "They're going to kill us all," Nick sighs.

One of the robbers places his mouth near Isabell's ear, then grabbed her butt. She figures she was going to be raped, and she tried to mentally prepare herself for it.

One of the robbers walked upstairs. Nick's grandmother was there, his Aunt Rosie, and his cousin, Gina with her two kids, Ben and Sam.

Rosie heard Gina scream and thought she was ill. She was sickly with a terminal disease. The robber ordered her to pick up the television in the room and to carry it downstairs. Gina complained that she couldn't lift it; the robber told her if she didn't, he'd kill her.

Isabella saw Gina struggling down the stairs with the television, the robber with the red hoodie pointing his gun at her. She felt so helpless; she was wondering how she could get her gun out of the car.

One of the gunmen ordered Gina to go down to the basement with him. Isabella figured he was going to rape her, she stood and faced them, "Gina you stay here, I'll go down there."

After Isabella stood and confronted the robbers, one of them said, "Everybody down into the basement."

Isabella was sure they were all going to die. Most cops have this feeling at least once in their cop lives. You tell yourself, "I can die on my feet or on my knees. I am not dying on my knees."

Isabella looked down the barrel of the gun and lunged toward the guy with the black hoodie and began to fight with everything she had. The black hoodie robber went flying toward the door as Isabella fought him. Nick jumped up and began fighting with the robber in the red hoodie.

Rose ran out the front door and as soon as the door slammed shut, she heard five shots. Rose ran to neighbors' houses, screaming for help, banging on doors, begging for someone to help her. Nobody would open their doors to her (city living at its finest).

Nick directed his attention to Isabella; she was down on the floor in a fetal position. The robber in the black hoodie was standing over her shooting her over and over.

Isabella looked down and saw blood on her shirt; she realized she had been shot in the chest. Nick felt an explosion in his neck and realized he'd been shot; blood was running onto his chest. The robbers ran out of the front door.

"Nick," Isabella said, "I can't breathe.

Sam, Gina's young son asked Nick if his mommy was okay. "She's okay, Sam, she just fainted," Nick replied. Sam was able to find a cell phone and makes a call to 911. Help was on its way.

It was becoming more difficult for Isabella to breathe; her eyes kept closing, and her head was dropping. EMS and the police were on the scene; it was chaotic, as it always is when a police officer is shot.

Isabella and Nick were taken out immediately and rushed to the hospital. Gina was DOS, dead on the scene, shot in the chest. Police officers were walking out, crying, most of them were friends and working companions with Isabella.

Sgt. Roger Englehardt, a city resident for his entire life, a mountain of a man, ex-professional boxer, dedicated and educated, nice guy, responded to the scene. He was in charge of the unit that is in charge of police shootings. He sent two detectives to St. Louis University Hospital to try to interview Nick and Isabella. They needed a description of the robbers/murderers.

Nick was shot three times; one of the bullets struck him below his ear and traveled through the back of his neck and hit his spinal cord. He was advised by medical personnel that they were not going to try to remove the bullet, that it could paralyze him.

A short time after the robbery a man went to the emergency room at Barnes Hospital for a bullet wound to his right hand. He stated he was shot during a robbery. He was wearing a red hoodie and he had gold teeth.

Officers responded to the ER. The shot man matched the description of one of the robbers. The officers walked outside and observed another man standing next to a car as if he was waiting for a friend; he had on a dark hoodie.

The guy got into the car and drove away. The police officers followed him to Forest Park; the driver threw something out of the car. It was a handgun. Officers arrested him. His name is Mario Coleman; the man inside of Barnes ER is Ledale Nathan.

Isabella was out of surgery and stabilized. Sgt. Roger Englehardt responded to the hospital and showed Isabella a photo lineup. She identified both subjects. They were charged with Murder in the 1st degree.

Mario Coleman's defense was that he was inside of the house at 902 Hickory, but Nathan was the man who killed Gina Stallis. Both robbers were sentenced to life without parole.

Nick and Isabella stopped dating but remained friends. Isabella was awarded the Medal of Valor, the highest award offered by the St. Louis Metropolitan Police Department.

Nick was involved in an auto accident and struck his head on the windshield. The bullet that was lodged near his spine popped out into his mouth. He spit it out and examined the projectile, went to an emergency room, and was assured he was going to be alright. Luck?

Isabella had/has permanent damage to her body from the bullets the inhuman robbers pumped into her. She was awarded a disability pension. She got on with her life.

Police officers rub elbows with a strange group of people, not just the criminals we encounter, but people who are interested in us as a group and as individuals. The friendship between Nick and Isabella was somewhat magical, maybe even scripted. A fireman meets a petite attractive policewoman on a call and they become friends, study together, and date. It ends in terror, tragedy, and life-changing events.

While Isabella moved on with her life, Nick did not. He was so traumatized that he turned to drugs for relief. He eventually lost his fireman job with the City of St. Louis; a good lifetime job, a job people compete for, and use outside influence to obtain, a job where the employee only works three days a week.

Nick needed money to survive; he robbed a bank and was incarcerated. The difference between a big-city cop and a big-city fireman. Cops fight criminals, firemen fight fires. The employee in both professions is indoctrinated to think of themselves as special. It's how we respond to danger, we're indestructible, chosen people.

It seems when one thing goes wrong the weak disintegrate. But that isn't the end of this horror saga. The guys who murdered Gina; shot Isabella, they went to prison, for life. But there are a hundred thousand of them walking and driving the streets of every major city in America with murder in their hearts and guns in their pockets.

14

CHAMP-ANDRIA V.M.

I am continuously amazed at how the media controls society. The unusual profession of the American cop draws people to it, spurred by films, detective television shows, nonfiction, and fiction books.

I, fresh out of the Marine Corps, anti-establishment, wild and uncontrollable, married without a job with a high school diploma and an honorable discharge, was enthralled with Clint Eastwood's Dirty Harry series, and Steve McQueen's Bullitt movie.
"I could do that", I mumbled to my bride, who actually had a job and supported me.

Bullitt was in 1969. I was hired by the St. Louis Municipal Police Department in 1970. I have not missed a paycheck since.

Andria Bitter and her boyfriend, Greg VanMierlo, had been together since their youth. They went to the senior prom together at Oakville Senior High School in far south St. Louis County.

Oakville is a paradise for middle-class people who work, save, and don't do stupid things. It's a family community where family/church and God come first. Residents here refer to Oakville as "The Island." It's partially surrounded by the Mississippi River and the Meramec River, to the north it is cut off by Interstate 255. After graduating from Oakville, Greg sold cars and Andria was a fitness coach Both of them desired to be cops.

St. Louis County was the place to become a cop in those ancient days. The city was a jungle and still is. Anyone who would strive to be a city cop is at the very least, confused, maybe delusional.

Greg had a relative who was killed in a robbery. It was in the city. So, both of them studied, worked, and waited until they were old enough to apply for the county cop job.

They both saw the movie, Lethal Weapon, several times. The scene where they do the takedown in the Christmas Tree lot impressed them, just like the chase scene in Bullitt impressed me. The media is in charge of our emotions. They push smoking, drinking, and other bad habits down our throats. If there's a shortage of cops, they make great cop movies for us to strive toward.

"I just want to put felons in jail," Andria advised me. Now the felons are putting cops in jail.

At the tender age of twenty-one, she was hired by the St. Louis County police. She graduated from the police academy in 2000, number one in her class in academics, physical training. Best overall recruit. She was the only female in her academy class; a few of the guys hated her. What guy wants to have his ass handed to him by a girl?

Andria was assigned to the fourth precinct, which is, The Island of Oakville, and Lemay. She patrolled in her hometown. There isn't a lot of crime in Oakville. Putting felons in jail there is a task. The radio calls consist of auto accidents, domestic disturbances in the evening watch, and shoplifters at the numerous storefronts on Telegraph Road. Cops have to dig for an arrest.

Andria is fit, smart, and attractive. New cops are assigned to a field training officer. These guys are usually good cops, steady and knowledgeable. Andria mentioned that her training officer drove with his hand on her thigh one time. She didn't object to the touching; I asked her why.

"Just dumb, I guess," she replied. She married Greg and he was hired by the county, went into the police academy, and hit the streets in the fourth precinct. Some male cops referred to Andria as "little lady", a display of ignorance she can't forget.

Andria set up a drug deal in sleepy Lemay (attached to the Island) at a 711 Convenience Store. A heroin dealer from the city was lured there by Andria on the premise of selling heroin. These dope dealers aren't bright and they don't want the dope, they want the cash the dope provides them.

So, the city heroin dealer shows up and Andria and her partner try to take him down. Her partner ends up being dragged by the dealer's car, so her partner shoots the guy a couple of times. Be advised, both Andria and her partner were in uniform, with marked police cars.

There's a pursuit that leads into the City of St. Louis (quagmire of criminals) where the heroin dealer crashes his car. Heroin dealer ends up dead. He had a cast on his leg and it was stuffed with packs of heroin.

Andria's road boss (her supervisor) was furious. Apparently, she didn't advise him of her plans. But in the cop business the cop never knows what's around the corner. Some deals work out, most don't.

Andria had set up an unauthorized sting, which in actuality was not covered by St. Louis County Police Department general orders. A new general order on stakeouts and surveillance was initiated. She got by with her over enthusiasm.

Andria patrolled in Oakville for approximately three years, with a partner she enjoyed working with; they scrambled to make felony arrests in sleepy Oakville. Rumors started by cop associates had them sleeping together. A former Marine cop friend of Andria's put a stop to the false rumors.

Andria desired to make a name for herself. It's why we're cops, to show off, be brave, and have people admire us. Of course, most guys admired Andria. She volunteered to fight in the annual Guns and Hoses fundraising event held every year the evening before Thanksgiving. It's always sold out; it is a contest of firemen and cops fighting it out toe to toe for three rounds.

There are cops in every police department who have had the experience of fighting in a ring with thousands of people in attendance. Boxing takes expertise and training, it is the "sweet science."

Tim Burke is a ring boxer, a Golden Gloves Champion, and a street fighter. He grew up Irish and tough in north St. Louis County. North County is where the working-class north St. Louis city folks moved to when their neighborhoods were given to the black masses living in squalor; in high-rise housing projects. They destroyed the projects; the northside homes were mostly brick, and the federal government, HUD, ran the white people out and to north St. Louis County.

Tim Burke's reputation was huge, and he was willing to fight for money. If there was a problem on a job site where Union Labor was involved, union leaders would hire Tim Burke to go to the worksite and rectify the problem.

Tim wasn't big, just tight and quick with a knockout punch in both hands; he was a wrestler, also. He had all of the moves to make him attractive to someone wanting revenge or protection.

When a group of men is together on work sites it is imperative that they do their jobs and get along with their coworkers. It isn't always that way. Tim was sent to a worksite in north county. A large obnoxious union member there was bullying the other workers. Tim was hired and he responded to the work site like a laborer.

Tim observed the ignorant laborer acting obnoxiously and bullying the other workers and Tim told him to stop. The guy got in Tim's face; Tim backed away and said, "Everybody gather around here, it's time for someone to learn a lesson in worksite etiquette.

The fool lunged at Tim and threw a big right hand. Tim dodged it and pummeled the guy down to the ground. Tim waited for him to get back on his feet. The guy swung again and Tim knocked him down again. The ignorant fool eventually limped to his pick-up truck and left the worksite. Tim's reputation grew, and he made somewhat of a living being a tough guy.

Vince Schoemehl, the Mayor of the City of St. Louis in the 1980s was a controversial guy. He stepped on everyone's toes; it was his schtick. He loved doing it. But Vince was gathering enemies, and he was receiving threats. He hired Tim Burke to be his security man, which meant if anybody screwed with Vince, Tim would kick their ass.

Tim accepted the position, and after being in the presence of a low-key, good guy, Tim Burke, Vince came to the realization that Tim Burke was/is quality people, a nice guy who deserved more out of life than being a fist for hire. Vince sponsored Tim Burke to become a City of St. Louis police officer. Mayor Vince had seen city cops for a lifetime, and in his mind, Tim Burke was head and shoulders a better candidate to be a cop than some city cops.

Tim was accepted and went into the police academy. He graduated and was a full-fledged city cop. It is an enjoyable job, or it was, not so much anymore with the "woke" generation.

An administrator wanted Tim to be an investigator; Tim was the kind of a guy people wanted to do things for. He told Tim of his plan. "What about the guy who's in that position now," Tim asked.

"We're going to move him out and move you in," the cop boss replied.

"I don't want it," Tim replied. Character had struck the St. Louis Metropolitan Police Department. Probably the only time.

St. Louis cops are probably the lowest paid cops in the region, and they do more work than any cops anywhere. The place is a breeding ground of criminals. Tim Burke applied for the St. Louis County Police Department. He was hired. He remained there; he was Andria's trainer and coach in the Guns and Hoses fights. With her inner strength and physical abilities, and with Tim Burke's training and coaching, Andria couldn't lose.

Andria's first fight was in 2002, she was assigned to the fourth precinct, and she fought Holly Knox, a Mehlville (south St. Louis County, but not The Island) firefighter. The fight went for three rounds, and Andria won every round. The twenty-thousand-plus crowd went crazy shouting and screaming Andria's name. She had class in the ring, and out of it.

Andria's second fight was in 2009. She fought Jennifer Stuhlman, a University City firefighter. Andria won all three rounds. In both fights, Andria stated that she started out slow but after the first time she got hit, she started fighting with everything she had and with the tools Tim Burke had given her. Andria said it was the coolest thing she had ever done. She loved it.

She said Jennifer Stuhlman was interviewed by the press before the fight and revealed that Andria was in St. Louis County narcotics. Andria was in an undercover capacity and it put a damper on her future assignments, but the county and Andria worked around it.

Andria advised that the men in the competition had separate locker rooms. The fighters did not have lockers, showers, or dressing rooms together. The women shared a locker room. There was no communication before or after the fights in the women's locker room, they barely looked at each other.

But Andria had just beat someone up in front of 20,000 people and now she had to shower and dress in front of the same person. It was awkward.

Fans (fanatics) and some cops, refer to her as "champ." She was gaining the notoriety she was seeking. Fame is fleeting but not for

Andria; she was living her dream. Her reputation is important to her. She guarded it continually. Her goal was to be the perfect cop; looks, intelligence, dedication. She demanded the respect of everyone, and she got it.

The Guns and Hoses event is a big deal in St. Louis. It's held at the Enterprise Center. It's sold out every year, and another two or three thousand people are standing. Andria was a huge draw.

The Backstoppers reaps the cash from the event. Usually over a million dollars a year. They assist family members of fallen cops and firemen. They are there to pay bills and provide for the survivors, and to aid the children of a line of duty death survivors until they are adults. Andria is the champ. I asked her how she felt about being called, "Champ."

"Embarrassed," she replied.

To the casual observer, narcotics would be insanely busy all of the time, but it isn't exactly like that. The narcotics detective is compelled to dig for every case. Informants are the key to a narcotics investigation. DEA and the FBI have big money for informants; local departments do not.

Andria did what every narcotics investigator must do, undercover buys. I couldn't imagine any drug dealer selling Andria drugs; she was blonde and blue and fresh, and she didn't get grungy. Her storyline was that she was buying drugs for her boyfriend, and it worked for her.

Every large police department has an Intelligence Unit. They're purveyors of information. They collect gossip for the Chief of Police, hopefully on his/her political enemies.

The rumor was started in the Intelligence Unit that Andria was a stripper in a strip joint on the eastside during her off-duty hours. Cops are brutal to their peers. She was a detective in the unit. The rumor started as a joke; there are no jokes in the cop game when it concerns a fellow cop's reputation.

I was a detective in the city's Intelligence Unit for eight years. Someone started the rumor that I was a drug dealer between the eastside and the west side. My home telephone was tapped, and my office phone in Intelligence and at my new job at DEA was tapped. Cop detective cars would drive past my house and jot down license numbers.

Even though Andria was a St. Louis County cop, much of her undercover drug buys were in the City of St. Louis, and most of them were buys from black guys. She was doing narcotics investigations and looking for a big case.

But Andria wasn't just buying from black guys; she bought dope from members of the Saddle Tramps outlaw biker gang. She also set up another sting of a lawyer, Thomas Noonan, the deputy mayor of the west county City of Kirkwood, Missouri.

Thomas Noonan had an oxycodone addiction. Andria had taken off a young girl on a search warrant who was selling meth. She was given the opportunity to work off her case by setting up other dopers, basically setting up her friends. She was so young she didn't have many friends to set up, so she asked one of her friends to help her.

Andria was introduced to the doper friend and she advised Andria that she could set up a rich politician (Tom Noonan) who was looking to purchase oxy. The gal set it up. The deal was going down on the parking lot of the South County Mall.

Andria and the doper gal were on the lot, waiting for Tom Noonan to show up. He drove up in a black Jaguar. The doper gal exited Andria's undercover car and walked to the Jaguar.

She advised Tom Noonan to give her the money up front and then they would go and get the oxy for him He agreed and gave her the cash. She exited the Jaguar and returned to Andria's undercover car. They drove off under the premise that they were going to obtain the drugs and return. Some other undercover detectives took Tom Noonan off.

The young meth dealer got a new lease on life. Tom Noonan's life was in shambles. He ultimately lost his law license, was prosecuted in state court and was given probation.

Whenever a defendant is arrested, unless he's a maniac, they are asked if they want to work for the cops. They're actually interviewed, like a job interview.

Some defendants lie, say they will, and then try to play both ends of the crime game. It never works. Information is spoon-fed to them to see if it gets shared with higher-up drug dealers. These druggies aren't smart enough to keep their mouths shut. The info filters back to the drug unit and the snitch druggie is rearrested and prosecuted. It's a nasty way to make a living.

In early 2009, the commander of the First Patrol Precinct in north St. Louis County complained to the drug unit commander that there was a motorcycle club, The Sin City Disciples, housed at Chambers and Diamond. He wanted the unit to investigate drug activity at that location. The drug unit started surveillance of the bike clubhouse.

Surveillance starts out with photos of the area, people coming and going, license numbers, and a dossier on the people seen on surveillance.

It's usually done from an undercover van discreetly placed near the property under surveillance, and periodically moved. After weeks of surveillance, the investigators start doing car checks/motorcycle/checks on people coming and going.

During surveillance, Andria did a stop on a black biker, Matthew Hunter. She had gotten information from a heroin proffer that Matt was wanted in Reynolds County for some traffic offenses. It had been a pursuit and the deputy pursuing him was the sheriff's daughter. He agreed to work for Andria if she could get him off on his out-of-county warrants. She did.

Another biker club was The Wheels of Soul which had a clubhouse at North Market and Vandeventer in the city. Both of these locations, north county and city were drug dens. Matt the snitch hit them hard; he was buying heroin, meth, and cocaine from bikers who were members of both the Sin City Disciples and the Wheels of Soul, one-percenter bike gangs, predominantly black.

Andria was detached to the local office of the FBI and worked the case federally. Her contact in the United States Attorney's Office was AUSA Sirena Wissler. Sirena was mesmerized by the picture-perfect Andria. Andria was 6% body fat, ran marathons for fun, and carried a Glock. AUSA Sirena was/is a beautiful fiery redhead who is a bulldog in the courtroom. They are friends for life.

There are several reasons for locals to take a case federal: Any proceeds from the case will go to the local police department initiating the case, which would be the St. Louis County Police Department. Asset forfeiture is a federal procedure.

Other reasons are, cash available to pay informants, which was the super snitch, Matt (he subsequently got wealthy off of the case), and jurisdictional problems; if a person is a fed, they can go across state lines and make arrests, seize assets, conduct electronic surveillance, and be assisted by other feds throughout the country.

Matt informed Andria that the black motorcycle gangs were spread throughout the country and were the biggest in Chicago. Andria subsequently hooked up with Special Agent Kevin Schuster, Alcohol Tobacco and Firearms in Chicago, Detective Mike Kennedy, Chicago Police Department, and Edward Gonzalez, Gary, Indiana Police Department.

Matt advised that the Sin City Disciples patched over to the Wheels of Soul gang, which meant they joined together. The patches these gangs use, are sacred to them. The Wheels of Soul Motorcycle gang was the biggest mixed-race gang in the country at that time.

In May of 2009, Matt advised Andria that St. Louis Chapter President Dominic Henley, a/k/a "Bishop" told his fellow Wheels of Soul that a member in Gary, Indiana had shot a Sin City Disciple. Bishop said the shooter was Jerry Peteet, a practicing attorney in Northwest, Indiana.

Andria confirmed that on May 28, 2009, a gunman had shot a victim in a dispute in a parking lot. This seemed like no big deal, but with the shooter being a practicing attorney in Gary, Indiana, and a member of the Wheels of Soul, there was federal interest.

This seemed on the surface that it was just another dispute between black bikers, and Peteet was indicted on the charge, but another man, Barry D. Rogers presented a document stating that he was the one who shot Robert "Damn Fool" Taylor.

Rogers said he was at the restaurant having a drink and socializing when Damn Fool Taylor entered the bar with a lady friend. Taylor was greeted by a man who gave him a friendly hug, but Taylor shoved the man into a table and the man fell to the floor.

The man got up and the two grappled before others broke them up. A security man and Peteet stepped between the men.

Peteet told the men he knew Taylor and that he has a mental problem and did not mean any harm to anyone. Taylor and his female companion left without any further incident, but Damn Fool had returned to the parking lot and was talking loudly and pacing.

Taylor walked up to Barry Rogers and another individual and they began to argue over personal issues. The argument got loud and Peteet came over and ordered his brother biker Damn Fool to leave. Damn Fool Taylor had a gun and he reached for it; Peteet pulled both of his guns and yelled at Taylor not to point his gun; Taylor pointed his gun and Barry Rogers fired a warning shot, then fired a second shot at Damn Fools leg which caused Damn Fool to drop his gun.`

Damn Fool Taylor fell, got up and ran to a car, and left the scene. He was shot in the hip. Rogers said he learned of Peteet's federal indictment for racketeering, attempted murder, and witness tampering, but Peteet didn't shoot Damn Fool, he did. Rogers had a burglary case pending in Indiana.

The battery case against Peteet was dismissed. Peteet is a member of the Wheels of Soul Motorcycle Gang. Damn Fool Taylor is a member of the Sin City Disciples. Peteet was a member of Sin City before he joined Wheels of Soul. It was obvious that Peteet drew up the affidavit for Rogers stating he shot Damn Fool Taylor.

In St. Louis, Matt the super snitch, "Mad Matt" as Andria and Sirena referred to him, was deeply undercover with the Wheels of Soul. He reported back to Andria and Sirena.

The Wheels started robbing other motorcycle gangs of their colors, and their armor, it's a religion to them, a brotherhood of sorts wherein the brothers kill one another to gain status. Another Wheels member, Kevin Berry was murdered on August 15, 2009.

Wiretaps were initiated throughout the United States. Drug transactions, plans, and sales were talked about via telephone. Dopers can't help themselves; there's so much money involved that they start out with their conversations, and then stop and say, "No business talk," and then two minutes into the conversation they go into the dope and murder business.

While wired, Mad Matt would record numerous conversations of their incriminating confessions of dope and murder, all the while the song Gangsta Party would be playing in the background.

In August of 2009, Matt was present when Bishop and other Wheels committed armed robbery, stealing colors from members of a local motorcycle club. Five days later, Bishop and fellow Wheel Timothy Balle, a/k/a "T" killed a Sin City Titans member.

Andria identified scores of Wheels members throughout the Midwest. Among them was Myron Ferris, a/k/a/ "Ghost," who was then Midwest Region President

Madd Matt was shipped to Chicago to work with ATF Agent Kevin Schuster. Matt purchased drugs and guns from Wheels members, seven times. The ATF and the Chicago Police Department provided an immediate boost to the case. S/A Schuster and CPD Officer Del Pearson shared crucial intelligence and hundreds of surveillance photos taken outside of The Wheels of Soul clubhouse. Matt made loads of drug and weapons buys from Wheels members.

As the investigations progressed, the list of targets grew longer. Chief among them was previously mentioned, Myron Ferris, a/k/a/ "Ghost." However, on July 17, 2011, "Ghost" was executed in his garage in Chicago, shot five times in the face.

Back in Chicago, two more Wheels were gunned down, Bryant Glass and Emmitt Suddoh. In Kentucky, Carlos Wesley Rose, a/k/a Pitbull, the only white guy indicted in the case, a corrections officer for the Kentucky State Reformatory, was arrested for racketeering and attempted murder in relation to the Wheels of Soul Motorcycle Gang.

The indictment of Rose alleges that Rose and other members of Wheels have been involved in a pattern of racketeering activity including the trafficking of cocaine and crack, murder, assault, attempted murder, robbery, conspiracy to commit murder, intimidation, arson, and kidnapping; since 2008 in Ohio, Missouri, Illinois, and Colorado; Andria initiated this indictment and arrest.

Javell Thornton was murdered in Marion, Ohio. Andria and Serena drove to the scene of the murder. Madd Matt witnessed this killing. It was as if the Wheels upper echelon were trying to eliminate anyone who could possibly be a snitch. Mad Matt was in their presence and they hadn't killed him. Andria and Sirena thought it was time to pull Mad Matt from the danger, but they didn't.

In January of 2011, several members of Wheels were involved in a shooting at the Hawks Motorcycle Club clubhouse in Chicago. Seven people were shot, and two, including Wheels of Soul member, Anthony Robinson, a/k/a/ "Blade" had been involved in the shooting. Wheels member Bryant Glass, a/k/a/ "Faith" was killed.

Five days after Bryant Glass, a/k/a/ "Faith" was killed, "Blade", later in the game, sold super snitch, Mad Matt, a forty caliber handgun. Ballistics revealed It was the same gun that had been used to kill Bryant Glass.

On January 10, 2011, the investigative team obtained a Title III wiretap on Wheels member Allan Hunter's cell phone. On January 29, 2011, Andria was monitoring the wire. Based on intercepted calls, she believed that several members of the Wheels of Soul were on their way to East St. Louis, Illinois (just across the Mississippi River from St. Louis, Missouri) intending to kill as many members of the Outcast OMG (another gang) as they could.

Andria alerted local law enforcement, who flooded the area. As a result, Wheels aborted the plan. Ultimately, Alan "Dog" Hunter admitted asking another Wheels member to make pipe bombs for an attack on another club, dealing in crack. Dog pleaded guilty.

While on the wiretap Andria did undercover work for the FBI. She had been officially trained by the Department of Justice two week undercover school and certified to work long-term FBI undercover cases to gain information on criminal groups across the United States.

The FBI undercover school is intense. Not everyone passes the curriculum.

She flew under an assumed name and infiltrated anarchist groups in North Carolina and South Carolina, and Texas. The federal government gets every ounce of talent out of every employee. While in St. Louis County Intelligence she did undercover work in the St. Louis region when the hippies and professional protestors would come to the region and protest against Monsanto. Girls with hairy armpits and guys with stinking beards.

Another Wheels member, Carlyle "Thundercat" Fleming pleaded guilty to the same charge, and admitted trying to kill two people, one with a firearm and one with a knife, to increase his status within the gang.

On March 6, 2011, Madd Matt attended a regional meeting of the Wheels of Soul in Marion, Ohio. Several hours later, Matt contacted Andria and advised her that he had just witnessed a shooting. He identified Anthony Robinson, a/k/a/ "Blade" as the shooter. Andria confirmed that three people had been shot, one fatally, at the Wheels clubhouse near Marion, Ohio .

Mad Matt was immediately removed from the Wheels of Soul case for his safety. Andria and ATF Agent Kevin Schuester began preparing for Grand Jury testimony, and assisted Matt in doing the same.

On June 9, 2011, after some twelve hours of testimony, the Grand Jury returned an indictment against eighteen defendants.

In June 2012, the Grand Jury returned a Superseding Indictment naming four new defendants, including Jerry Peteet, a/k/a/ "Angel". He was arrested at the Lake County (In) Courthouse where he was preparing to go to court to defend a client.

As the investigators interviewed cooperators, they learned that Anthony Robinson, a/k/a/ "Blade" had shot and killed an off-duty Corrections Officer in Chicago on November 1, 2009 following a Halloween party.

Phone calls from the Cook County Jail, during which Robinson warned a fellow Wheel to destroy any evidence linking them to "Halloween" were documented as evidence.

Sixteen of the twenty-four Wheels of Soul defendants pled guilty. The eight remaining defendants proceeded to trial beginning on October 15, 2012. The trial involved roughly sixty witnesses and over 500 exhibits. It was punctuated by rumored death threats, resulting in the United States Marshalls' Protection Service for the lead trial attorney and her family.

Despite the courtroom drama, the Marshalls Service masterfully managed every defendant (18) and witnesses (60) , with not a single incident during the eight-week trial.

Andria's case, which started with surveillance and a traffic stop of the super snitch, Mad Matt, resulted in the conviction of twenty-two men in the Eastern District of Missouri and two others in the Northern District of Illinois.

They were convicted of offenses including Racketeering, Conspiracy, Murder, Attempted Murder, Conspiracy to Commit Murder, and Conspiracy to Distribute Crack Cocaine.

Anthony Robinson, a/k/a/ "Blade" was sentenced to three consecutive life terms, plus 360 months.

Other sentences ranged from forty-six months to 276 months. The investigation resulted in the purchase of over 300 grams of crack, and the purchase/recovery of more than fifty firearms.

Portions of the above narrative were gleaned from a United States Attorney's award ceremony descriptor.

Andria was awarded the Distinguished Service Award by the United States Attorney. Other law enforcement investigators also received the award: Major Bill Collins, Marion, Illinois Police Department, Corporal Edward Gonzalez, Gary, Indiana Police Department, Detective Sinclair Harley, Gary, Indiana Police Department, Detective Jeff Hornyak, Gary, Indiana Police Department, Detective Jerone Jackson, St. Louis Metropolitan Police Department, Detective Devinn Jones, Chicago, Illinois Police Department, Detective Isaac Lambert, Chicago, Illinois Police Department, and Police Officer Del Pearson, Chicago, Illinois Police Department

Detective Michal Kennedy, Chicago Police Department, was, later in his career, shot in the line of duty and was given a disability retirement. Andria is still in touch with him.

ATF Special Agent Kevin Schuster has since died from alcohol poisoning, a federal law enforcement catastrophe that is epidemic. AUSA Sirena Wissler is still toiling for our rich uncle.

Andria was on a roll. She had proven to everyone that she was the "champ" in the Academy, in uniform patrol, in undercover drug assignments, in the Guns and Hoses boxing ring, and in huge federal nationwide investigations.

But you can't satisfy everyone. There are other female and male cops in the St. Louis County Police Department. Some are catty; some are jealous, and some can't wait to disrespect/hate someone like Andria who, in most ways, is infallible.

She was out there alone, carrying a huge perfect reputation; people love to shoot down stars; it's a sport in places like police departments. She was a gorgeous gal/cop with a great resume. Now what?

But before the naysayers, the haters, and the backstabbers could get their knives and arrows into Andria's back, Andria got a telephone call. It was from the personnel division of Monsanto Chemical Company. They wanted to know if she would be interested in working for them in the capacity of Executive Protection Security Specialist.

The Board of Directors of Monsanto mandated that their executives while traveling, have protection. In a cop's mind, this is an honor to be chosen for such an assignment. We're aglow with anticipation. There's status and more money.

Andria contemplated the new job offer. She'd just finished the huge interstate drug case, spent six weeks in a federal trial, and in her mind, there wasn't much that could match that experience.

Greg liked the extra money aspect. She took the job. She was no longer a St. Louis County cop detective.

I asked Andria how the Monsanto Corporation found out about her. "I don't know, I guess it's because I have a good reputation," she replied

15

Daph & THE BRAIN

JAN FORE & MANAGEMENT MONSTERS

Daphne Allen came from Kentucky to the big city of St. Louis trying to find herself. She wasn't a petite little cutie like some of the cop-gals, she was tall, maybe 5'10, and she was full-breasted. Daphne was warm and friendly, sexy, feminine, and smart. Of course, all of the new cop gals were smart and sexy.

Daphne had a boyfriend before joining the police department and he owned a nightclub/tavern in south St. Louis County, near The Island of Oakville. Daphne tended the bar and was part owner.

She wore revealing clothing and acted out the part of a sexy barmaid while watching every cent that went over the bar and into the cash register. It has to be that way in the bar business. Free drinks, and pilfering by employees, puts the entrepreneur into bankruptcy.

Daphne and her boyfriend split. She got nothing for her toils in the bar. She was strong enough to turn her back on both experiences. Daphne's dad was a cop in the St. Louis area. She had mentioned to him and her mom that she was considering becoming a cop in St. Louis.

Her dad forbade it. That's all it took for Daph. She took the test, scored high, passed the background investigation, and was on her way to the police academy. After graduation, she was sent to the fourth police district.

I was still a cop, and had over thirty years on the job. I was sent to the fourth district and placed at Historic Union Station as a beat cop. The station was actually a parking lot with fast-food restaurants, some good restaurants, storefronts selling clothing, a tourist destination for visitors to purchase junk as gifts, and parking for hockey games and basketball tournaments. The parking was a cash business and the owners of the station made gobs of cash. It's the reason Union Station is continually sold and remodeled. It is a cash cow. It's an aquarium now.

There were black gangs hanging and roaming around inside of the station and outside in the parking lot. I was obligated to rid this tourist stop of these ne'er do wells. I recognized the draw for the gangs; it was a neat place, and perfect for them to take over, which is what they did.

I studied the situation, and over a two-year period, basically ran the gangs out of the station. I was fighting much of the time with young black gangsters, rolling around on the hard floor, fighting and having my picture taken by people going to the hockey games just down the street; I was 56 years old.

Most of the cops in the fourth district avoided Union Station. It was trouble, which meant that I was mostly on my own, except for some private security guards employed by the station. There were a couple who I could/would trust.

I recognized some of the problems there. Marijuana was being sold over the counter at a couple of fast-food restaurants. I had made some arrests, which always meant chasing some young black dude down, wrestling with him, pounding with my fists, spraying with pepper spray, and arresting him.

Pepper spray (mace) gets on the person using it as well as the guy getting it. I would lay in bed after a long night at the station (6 p to 2 a) and not sleep because of the burning sensation of the mace.

It was tough for an old cop. The establishment that ran the station was made aware of the restaurants selling weed over the counter. It was making tons of cash from weed sales.

I asked the guy in charge who owned the restaurants. That information was not available to him. The guy Steve Miller, a St. Louis staple in the crooked business dealings part of St. Louis society, hired two felons to run the security department. They were enemies of mine. One of them was someone who the I had dealings with when I was detached to the Drug Enforcement Administration.

Things got dicey when those two took over. The one who was an ex-con was fired after I complained to Captain Larry O'Toole (chapter-4-fame) about him and Captain Larry demanded that he be removed from the station. But a precarious situation got more precarious. Steve Miller wanted me out of there.

Larry O'Toole wasn't a cop supervisor who was going to be bossed around. He threatened to remove me and not replace me. So, I was in limbo at Union Station. Basically, I rode my cop bicycle alone in the downtown area and if anything happened at the station I would respond.

Enter Daphne Allen. Daph had been monitoring the Union Station fiasco, as most of the fourth district cops had; she volunteered to be part time partner. We had fun together riding our Trek 21-speed mountain bikes around the downtown area. On the day watch, we'd ride the whole district. On warm summer nights, we'd take longer rides.

One summer evening I asked Daph to join me for a ride on the bike path by the Mississippi River. It was pitch black and out of our assigned area. We headed out, our bicycle headlights showing us the path. There were always transients, homeless, armed robbers, and murderers lurking on the bike path, especially at night, but being cops and armed we didn't worry. We were the only ones on the path.

We were way out of our assigned area, all the way to the 6th police district, maybe two miles away from downtown St. Louis. We turned around and headed back. My rear tire went flat.

"I've got a flat," I advised Daph. We stopped and tried to figure out what to do. There was a beat car at our bike office with a bike rack on the back. "Daph," I continued, "Go to the beat office and get the car with the rack. I'll start walking my bike and I'll meet you when you get the car." She reluctantly did.

I walked in the darkness; there was brush and old buildings between me and the Mississippi and I strained to try to get a look into the darkness. I couldn't see anything, which meant that if someone was in the brush or one of the dilapidated buildings, he could see me. Although the headlight on the bike was on, I'd have to turn the bike toward a noise to see who or what was coming out of the brush.

So, I walked and pushed my bike. After about ten minutes, I could see a light coming toward me; it was Daph. "I couldn't leave you all alone out here," she said. "I called for John LaPlante to get the beat car and to meet us."

That's the kind of working relationship I had with Daphne. We ate together, shopped together, and at times did police work together.

The downtown area in St. Louis has exclusive apartment buildings, but surprising was the types of people who flock to these apartments. Some of the apartments have Mississippi River views, which in reality the apartment dweller is looking across the river at the slum of East St. Louis, Illinois. Most have city lights views. The dwellers are just like the average neighborhoods within the city, dangerous, desperate people.

The bike unit is sometimes called to domestic disturbances, neighbor disputes, and theft reports, but there must be a safe place for the bike cops to secure their bicycles. They're bought and paid for by the Downtown Partnership, and they are expensive.

The old Mansion House Apartment building has security for our bikes. Daph and I answered a call there for a neighbor dispute. We secured our bikes, took the elevator to the 8th floor, and went to the door of the caller.

We banged on the door and said "PO-LICE just like we would in the ghetto of North St. Louis. We heard a familiar sound, the slide of an automatic weapon being pulled backward and released. That meant someone chambered a round into a chamber of a semi-automatic weapon.

Daph pulled her Berretta nine-millimeter pistol, I left mine holstered. I'd been on disturbance calls for 34 years, and where I was once assigned most citizens answered the door with a gun in their hand.

I figured the guy behind the door was just signifying; if he'd wanted to shoot a cop, he'd already had it cocked and hidden on his person. One thing about a cop going through a door with a gun in his hand is that it hinders you from defending yourself, fighting, or grappling for your cop life. It narrows the field of self-defense; your only choice is to shoot the drunk or drugged fool.

The guy you are about to talk to figures you're not going to shoot him, but if the man cop only has one hand readily available to him, he might try to kick your ass. Everybody is crazy when they call the cops.

The door opened and there stood this guy with an automatic in his hand. Daph had her muzzle pointed at his heart. "Put the gun on the floor and back away from it," I calmly ordered him.

He hesitated but did as he was told. I retrieved the weapon, took out the clip, cleared the weapon, and placed it in my belt. The complainant told us the guy in the apartment across from him had threatened him, and that he was in fear of his life.

There was another man in the apartment, watching us, and there was an infant lying on the couch, sleeping. I thought about the scenario. Gunfire can lead to anything, bullets flying through windows, through walls, maybe into an infant.

The complainant was intoxicated and the other man appeared to be, also, but he did not utter a word while we were there. I placed the retrieved pistol on a shelf in the living room, and the clip behind the bar. The guy never observed me doing this.

We listened to this guy's spiel about his neighbor, and finally, we advised him we would talk to him. We walked out, knocked on the door across from the apartment, and were met by another intoxicated man. He was advised to stay away from his neighbor. He agreed; Daph and I were riding again.

Daph dated a couple of cops, but there was nothing serious happening romantically with her. She met a downtown detective, Dave Bonenberger; Dave was smitten with Daph, but Daph was cautious. So, they dated and had fun together.

Dave was a mechanical genius. He rode and worked on Harley Davidson Motorcycles. Cops ride Harley's. It's almost a trademark for cops. Harley's almost always need something mechanical done to them. Dave was always busy fixing some cop's Harley.

Dave rode with cops off-duty. He and a dozen or so city cops would meet up and ride from bar to bar in the city it was a bike gang but without the drama of other bike gangs. They were cop friends. They wore cop/bike/club/ colors, and some of them wore snazzy little helmets, like the ones worn by infantry soldiers in WW1, cute to look at but ineffective.

On one summer evening, the cop/bike/gang/ friends were motoring around in Soulard and Dave crashed his Harley. He went flying and his cute little helmet split apart and he received some head trauma. He was in the ER and one of his buddies telephoned Daph. She responded and his buddies, who were concerned about Dave consoled her, told her they loved her, and all of that close-knit-cop rhetoric that means nothing, but sounds good when it's delivered by a drunk cop.

Another cop responded; a captain, (from the Jan Fore story) who was now assigned to the office of the Chief of Police. He hated Dave Bonenberger or anyone who was friends with Jan Fore. He advised the area sergeant, John Frank, to have a sobriety test done on Dave Bonenberger. John Frank refused the order. Dave was released to return home with Daphne.

Sadly, cops receive head trauma far too often. It's one of the perils of the job (divorce and alcoholism are among them) and Dave didn't need any more trauma to his big brain. He laid off riding for a while, but fixed his buddy's bikes.

Dave proposed to Daph, and she accepted. Daph never did anything halfway in her life. She wanted a big wedding, and she wanted two honeymoons in Jamaica, one with all of her friends and some of her family, and then one with just Dave and her.

It happened, big wedding, big trip. Daph paid for some of her friends to join she and Dave. A few told her they would pay her back; but never did. It didn't matter to Daph. She loved her cop friends, and she loved her younger sister, who at that time was single, smart, and cute.

After the wedding and the honeymoons, Daph rented a banquet room in a restaurant in Soulard and invited about twenty of her closest friends. I was there with my wife. It was a catered affair and was first class.

I kept reflecting back to Big-Bob and Rochelle (RoRo the PoPo). I was getting close to cops again, something I was reluctant to do, especially female cops.

Big-Bob was with me in the bike unit at this time, and I figured he was concerned about any close friendships with female cops.

The close friendship continued, Daph stayed in the bike unit and I retired. I speak with Daph about once every 10 years. She and Dave purchased a house in south St. Louis (cops were required to live within the city limits) and Dave fixed it up; remodeled the kitchen and the bathrooms and did his genius thing to it.

Dave was promoted to sergeant, Daph got pregnant and everything was going along fine. Dave became the President of the Police Officers Association and he fixed Harley's on the side.

Dave was an ambitious fellow, and he desired to be the assistant director of the police academy. The position was open, and Dave was more than qualified, so Dave asked the Director of the academy, Lieutenant Mike Muxo if he could be considered for the position.

Mike Muxo is a mountain of a man, a martial arts expert who grew up in Miami, Florida, and was a street kid. He was also a good athlete and star football player. He went to college, played college ball, graduated, and then got a job at a Missouri college near St. Louis as an assistant coach.

The college (Hootie Owl College) was a diploma mill that city cops attended and graduated from without ever attending classes. It folded leaving Mike Muxo unemployed. He applied to the city police department and was hired.

Mike was a cop to be promoted. He was put in charge of the academy gymnasium, taught self-defense classes, and was a lecturer. He was intense and still is. Mike was promoted to sergeant and lieutenant and was the academy director with very little street experience, but he was intimidating and serious, and someone (cop leader) figured his demeanor was good for the police recruits to identify with. He was a natural looking bully; an average man's worst nightmare, but actually nonviolent.

Muxo advised Dave that the job was going to be filled by a black female, one of Lieutenant Colonel Reggie Harris' friends, end of the story.

Muxo then advised Dave to not apply for the position of assistant director in an email because he'd be wasting his time; the fix was in (hard evidence). Dave applied for the assistant director job, anyway, and he wrote Muxo an email stating that he had.

At a crime scene, Muxo approached Dave and asked him to go into an alleyway with him. He advised Dave that Lieutenant Colonel Reggie Harris, one of the deputy chief's, who is African American, ordered Muxo to "bring color down to the academy." And if Dave didn't make a fuss, he could expect to still land a good position in the future.

The job was given to the black female. In Dave's mind, the assistant director of the academy was Dave's dream job. Most cops, including me, would have buckled under. The cop job is political; people in charge desire that their friends work for them. Dave, is a smart guy, and I'm an average guy.

There are so many job openings within the police department, great investigative positions, spy jobs, being detached to federal agencies (a cop could spend most of his career working for the feds and still be a city cop, never showing up at the department or wearing a uniform) and the pay is much more, with an undercover car, but Dave (genius) saw substance within his grasp.

Dave hired an attorney and sued the police department, Muxo, and Reggie Harris. Life went on and the case went to federal court, it was for Reverse Racial Discrimination. Dave won a cash settlement of $650,000, plus $175,000 for his attorney fees which went to the State Supreme Court and was upheld, (St. Louis Post Dispatch article and interview with Dave Bonenberger).

Muxo was sent to a district, and Dave was transferred to the same district and was working for Muxo. Dave complained and then was placed into a job where he had nothing to do and no one to supervise. He was a sergeant without men. That brilliant idea came from the new Chief of Police, Doyle Dotson. There is something called retaliation from a lawsuit. Dave spoke to his attorney.

Daphne, who by then had a job investigating landlords and troubled properties within the city was concerned she would be targeted; the department did not harass her. Dave sued again, this time for retaliation, and was awarded a $750,000, settlement

Daphne was allowed to retire with a twenty-year pension. Dave stayed on and eventually retired with a twenty-three-year pension. They're living a good life in another state. Dave is The Director of Security for a Cannabis company.

Muxo's still fighting the battle at the police department. Reggie Harris is retired.

Jan Fore was the poster child for the new female cop joining the St. Louis Metropolitan Police Department, cute, smart, athletic, searching for something, someone, and not knowing what or who.

We are indoctrinated that our captain, our commander, is a person to be loved and respected. His/her decision is the gospel, and many cops adhere to the rule that the captain is wise, correct and no one else is.

It is a magical rank; the big-city captain is basically immune to harsh disciplinary procedures. Some get into trouble and even are suspended, but they get their jobs back, with back pay, and civil judgments in their favor.

Softball is a political game within the St. Louis Metropolitan Police Department. Good players are revered as much as St. Louis Cardinal baseball players. Cop Gods, and softball Gods, are synonymous in St. Louis.

Jan Fore met a police captain, a commander of a western district, at a bar after a police department softball game. He was a softball hero. He was on the fast track to becoming the Chief of Police, someday. He was ambitious and smart, but he lacked extreme political backing for the job.

He and Jan Fore began dating. He was married and had children. Jan was single and needy. It was apparently a torrid relationship and it lasted for months. They traveled together, took vacations to Cancun, and, were an item in the police department.

Jan was assigned to the third police district, a busy southside district with the brewery as its cornerstone. Jan's coworkers loved her and many advised her to stay away from this married captain. She was counseled by her peers but did not heed their advice.

Coworkers visiting her house on Rutgers Street observed photos of them in Cancun, and several other photos of them enjoying life together while the captain's wife sat at home and felt everything was alright in their marriage.

The captain was in the slow process of splitting with Jan Fore. These big-screen romances usually lose steam after a while. The guy decides he's going to be true to his wife, again, or some such rationalization. The guy figures he can go back to mommy and live a clean life. He hates the mistress for seducing him, even though she is the victim of the crime.

The mistress (Jan and so many like her) thinks they are in love with the cheating dude. What they don't realize is that the cheater is a pimp and he has made the mistress a whore. There's no going back for either of them.

On a brisk September day in 1992, Jan Fore didn't show up for work. As is usually the case, there is a concern, so the watch commander sent a car by her house to check on her well-being.

The front door was ajar, and one of the officers, Matt Hanewinkel was the cop. He opened the door and observed Jan lying on the couch in the living room; she had shot herself with her department nine-millimeter Beretta pistol and had apparently been lying there for hours.

Matt called for a supervisor and then perused the house. He had been in the house before and had observed vacation photos of Jan and the Captain on the fireplace mantel. The photos were gone.

The telephone receiver was still near her hand, off the hook, and an investigation by Matt was that she had apparently shot herself during the telephone conversation.

Speculation was that whomever she was talking to knew she had shot herself, came to the house, walked in, and observed her body. That person then removed the Cancun photos, and or any evidence relating to a romance with Jan, left the residence, and didn't close the door. The hair of the dog.

End of a problem for the captain; he was free to resume his life as if nothing had ever happened. In fact, this type of activity within the department wasn't looked down upon. But he was concerned this incident might have a negative bearing on any more promotions for him. The captain had priorities.

The incident drew the attention of another cop who was intent on becoming the chief of police. This guy was backed by Pipefitters Local 562 (the gangster trade union from chapter # 1) and he is as rotten as the captain. He'd been a lifelong hound dog.

Our pay raises were granted by the State Legislators, and 562 had a state senator and a state representative as card-carrying members of 562. The union guys would contact the chief of police and advise him that if he wanted pay raises for his troops, he'd have to promote the union friends. It worked every time.

So, the little dog consoled the captain and they made a pact. The little star would help him gain rank with him if he agreed to be in servitude to him. The gangster trade union determined who was going to be promoted within the St. Louis Metropolitan Police Department.

They also had a member of the Board of Police Commissioners as a close friend. They chummed around together, and played golf regularly. Little dog didn't golf, but he would occasionally ride in the golf cart.

The captain agreed to declare his loyalty to the little dog and eventually retired with rank. The little dog became the chief, retired, or was forced out for being a crook, but they all lived happily ever after.

Except for Jan Fore's mom and dad, and the cop coworkers who loved her and were always concerned about her. As a group, they anonymously sent a letter to the department's Internal Affairs Division asking for an investigation into her death. Of course, nothing ever came from it.

The beat goes on, on and off of the beat.

16

LIZ BAKER

THE CUTEST COP/GAL

Liz Baker was around city cops most of her life; her mom had some health problems and the police had to be called to the family apartment in south St. Louis occasionally. There was no man or dad, or anyone to take care of Liz and her sister.

Liz would beg the city cops to not hand her and her sister over to Child Protective Services. She assured the cops that she could care for them until her mom got readjusted and returned home. The cops didn't call Child Protective Services. Liz, by hook or crook, kept the family together.

Liz was smart and a good student. She eventually attended Rosati-Kain, an all-girls Catholic High School in the CWE. After high school, she attended various local colleges seeking a degree.

Liz didn't aspire to be a city cop; she needed a job, and she went to the police department personnel division to apply for a job as a dispatcher. This was in the late 90s and the city was actively searching for cop candidates.

The interviewer asked her why she wasn't applying for a police officer's position. She didn't think she was qualified. She was persuaded to take the police officer's entry test, passed it, and a background investigation was conducted. She was hired and went to the police academy.

After graduation, she was sent to the third district, the south patrol, which she'd be patrolling in her home district. Like all new cops, Liz loved the job. And being super attractive, the cops loved her.

She dated cops; one, in particular, Officer Clay, was smitten with Liz, and Liz liked him, so they dated steadily. The city police department had/has no rule against employee dating. It's an open game atmosphere, married or nonmarried, cops date.

Liz and Officer Clay were both young, and single, although Officer Clay had her by about six years. If some other cop asked Liz out, Officer Clay would advise them that Liz was spoken for. There were so many young and cute cop/gals in the police department that it wasn't a big deal.

So, Officer Clay and Liz were an item. Officer Clay was/is a lady's man. He's a handsome country boy from southern Illinois, and smooth with the ladies. He swooned Liz for several years as the two of them fought to stay alive in the city of St. Louis while carrying a badge and a gun.

Officer Clay always wanted to return to country living. There were outlying police departments wanting to hire seasoned city cops. Finding the right one was difficult. But working in the city and being forced to live in the city was annoying to him.

Cops, especially young cops, pine for a detective position. They want to be famous investigators. The steps to a specialized unit within the St. Louis Police Department are clearly outlined in cop special orders. An officer must have three years on the job before he/she is chosen to be assigned to a specialized unit. This rule is abused daily; if you have influential friends, the Chief's Office will detach the cop to a specialized unit.

It galls most cops when someone with six months on the job is transferred downtown to a detective unit, given a desk and a department detective car to take home while the cops without pull do the dirty job of district work.

Officer Clay stayed in patrol, but Liz was asked if she wanted to be on the Mounted Patrol (ride horses.) She was leery of the job, but she took it. She started the training, which is rigorous, and was having a difficult time.

Part of the mounted training is riding bareback; the horse and the rider are one. The Mounted Patrol is a public relations dream; the horses are beautiful; the cops are horsemen, trained and confident, and the horses do what they are trained to do. What better person to have on the Mounted Patrol than a mixed-race, gorgeous, petite-in-shape, female cop?

When Liz rode bareback, she would raise her right arm as if she was balancing herself. It was, in the eyes of the trainers, unprofessional and unattractive. The job was acting 101, show off, you're cute and a cop, and riding a horse for the public.

Liz was advised to not hold her arm up and to stop trying to balance herself. She tried, to no avail, so a trainer had a bright idea. He took crime scene tape and tied her arm to her body. She subsequently fell off of the horse at a full gallop. Best laid plans of mice and men.

Liz was a little girl and she was injured. She couldn't get back on that horse. She was under a doctor's care, and eventually went back to the third district. Officer Clay was still assigned to the first district (same building) and they decided to get married.

It was not an elaborate wedding; close friends and family; Liz and Officer Clay were already living together, but they were both becoming disillusioned with the city police department and city living.

A close friend of theirs, Officer Robert Stanze II, was shot and killed in the line of duty. Officer Stanze had arrested a suspect who had shot another officer. Officer Stanze handcuffed the suspect and did a cursory search, then placed him in the backseat of the police car.

The suspect had a pistol hidden in his waistband, and he was able to obtain it while he was sitting in the backseat. Officer Stanze was standing next to the police car; the suspect was able to grab his pistol and shoot through the window with it while handcuffed behind his back.

Officer Stanze, who was wearing a bulletproof vest, was struck in the side and the bullet entered his torso between the two parcels. Officer Stanze's partner opened fire on the suspect, wounding him. Officer Stanze had six years in the police department. He was married and his wife was pregnant with twins. It's a rough job, reader friend.

The Stanze shooting plagued Liz and Officer Clay. Officer Clay had been talking to far west police department personnel divisions, in St. Charles County, Missouri. There was land out there; it was country, he and Liz could build a house, or purchase one on some property and live their lives.

Liz contributed the money she got from the city police department, and they both resigned and moved to Lincoln County. Liz gave Officer Clay the pension money she had paid into her city pension.

The country police department hired Officer Clay. But this department wasn't lenient like St. Louis. There's a clause stating that anyone related could not be employed by the police department.

That meant Liz would have to search for a job in another department. She eventually was hired by Lincoln County. They lived in Troy, Missouri, in a house with land, had two kids and life went on.

Her desk in Lincoln County Sheriff's Department had a place for her daughter to come to after school and do her homework. When Liz went back to the road, she worked straight nights so she could be at home with the kids, or when they came home from school.

The years sped by; she and Officer Clay weren't seeing much of one another; they worked opposing shifts. They argued but didn't yell or scream. Finally, Officer Clay told Liz he wanted a divorce.

He had been in a romantic relationship with another female cop and had been for two years. Hair of the dog. She was also married, and twenty-five years younger than him. Liz was shocked. She didn't have any idea that there was another woman.

They separated and Officer Clay kept the farm. Liz moved back to St. Louis and got a job in security at Washington University. She was a campus cop. But in retrospect, it was a good thing. Her children were able to attend Washington University at a discounted rate, and with scholarships, it was a bargain.

The divorce dragged on. Officer Clay, who by then was Sergeant Clay, abandoned the family home. It was burglarized and vandalized. He stopped making the mortgage payments. Luckily, Liz had a relative who was in the real-estate business. She sold the farm for a short sale. They got no equity out of the place. All of the money Liz had in her life was used to buy the farm.

Liz was still suffering from the horse accident. The divorce dragged on for six years. Sergeant Clay had the divorce papers, but he didn't sign them. Liz was under mounting pressure, and she suffered a stroke. Hospitalized and bewildered, she was forced to take a disability retirement. Her grown children are successful, educated, and smart.

Liz lives in an efficiency apartment in the Central West End. She has no car, so she walks where ever she has to go. I asked her if she still carried a gun. "No," she replied, "I sold my gun and my wedding rings to pay my daughter's registration fee for her high school." Liz is forty-nine years old. She's alone in the world.

Sergeant Clay is now Lieutenant Clay, still a cop. He and the married female cop divorced their spouses at the same time. Her husband found out about their affair because she had a picture of Clay in her nightstand drawer.

17

Jenna Diehl Christian

DEATH RIDE

Jenna Diehl Christian grew up in University City, a suburb of the City of St. Louis, Missouri. At age eleven, her parent's thought being so close to the city (St. Louis) was not good for their children they were right. The city was/is dangerous; University City was/is dangerous. It's where Washington University is; it has a vibrant shopping area, nightlife, and restaurants.

Jenna's parents moved the family to Augusta, Missouri, approximately fifty miles from the danger of the big city; it was in the middle of nowhere, but it was quiet and safe. Jenna would beg to go back to the city with her older sister who had a driver's license and access to a car.

One of her favorite memories was a visit to the forbidden city with her sister and her high school friends. For some reason, they ended up in a parking lot in beautiful, and safe, Clayton, Missouri, another suburb of St. Louis.

There was a Clayton police officer in the parking lot, and Jenna started talking with him. The police officer was nice to Jenna, and he allowed her to look inside his police car. He answered her questions and smiled at her. She was fascinated with cops.

When she was a freshman in high school she joined a Police Explorers Post in Washington, Missouri. She was in love with the experience. She wasn't popular and didn't have many friends, but the Explorer Post made her feel like she was part of a team, and the officers were like family.

The Explorer Post traveled and competed in law enforcement competitions, and the group did really well. Jenna was good at the competition and won several leadership awards. The Explorer's Post helped to define her and she grew up in the program. She knew she wanted to be a cop and she made it clear to everyone in her life.

Jenna's parents always supported her; they didn't think she would actually become a cop. In her senior year of high school, she met Scott Christian, a part-time cop in Augusta. Scott had applied to be a cop in the City of St. Louis and he was waiting to be hired. Scott was hired by the city in 1999; Jenna went to college for a couple of years but didn't earn a degree. She left school and married Scott when she was twenty.

As soon as she turned twenty-one, Jenna applied to the City of St. Louis, which was in August of 2000. She was hired, finished the academy, and was sent to the fourth district. She was assigned the 6:00 p.m. to 2:00 a.m. shift and was riding with Mike Barwick most of the time, both new/young officers.

On August 29th, 2002, Jenna and Mike Barwick went to roll call at Central Patrol; roll call isn't like it was when I was a young cop. There were about forty cops at roll call. They played poker before roll call, grab assed, and insulted each other. Sometimes they'd fistfight over a district girl. Now there are two or three cops and one supervisor at roll call. If a cop is five minutes late, they will dock their pay. After roll call, they trudged to their police car. Jenna wanted to drive; Mike had the keys. Mike told Jenna that if she could get to the keys before him, she could drive. Mike tossed something out into the parking lot; Jenna thought it was the keys to the police car so she ran after them.

It wasn't the car keys; Mike laughed as he slid into the driver's seat and started the car. Jenna slid in, shotgun, and was laughing with him. The evening went on, uneventful, and they were talking to another cop in a car (car to car) at Madison and 20th.

Things changed drastically (Jenna doesn't remember what happened but she read the police report).

"There was a little gas station across the street from where we were. Mike noticed a car there and started creeping toward it, close enough to get the plate. I called out the plate, but before we could get the plate back from the dispatcher, the chase was on. The police report states we were northbound on 25th Street, following a stolen car, and entered the intersection of 25th and St. Louis Avenue, traveling at about eight-two miles per hour when the driver's side of the police car was T-boned by a car traveling eastbound on St. Louis

Avenue. The police car slid sideways, hit the curb, and started flipping; the car caught on fire in the engine compartment and passenger side. They were able to get me and Mike out before the flames completely took over the car."

Sergeant Dave Bonenberger was one of the officers who pulled Jenna and Mike out of the burning police car.

Jenna continues, "I woke up in the hospital several days after the accident, to my mom telling me I was ok. My mom, Dad, and Scott were all sitting around me. They told me Mike had died. Mike's parents came to my room, but I was pretty out of it. I couldn't attend the funeral; I couldn't understand why, if I had medical people around me, I should've been able to attend the funeral. I slept a lot."

It should be noted, reader friend; when an officer is injured on duty, a police officer is assigned to sit with them, twenty-four hours a day, until they are ambulatory. Officer Donna Wisdom sat with and talked with Jenna during her hospital stay.

Donna is a veteran female police officer; she'd been through a lot in the department; she got pregnant by a married police officer and she bounced around the districts until she got assigned to the bicycle unit in the fourth district. She and I worked together; she is quality people. She is best friends with Daphne Allen.

Donna stated, "Sitting with Jenna and talking with her made me look at things a little differently and made me gain a whole lot of respect for her and her strength."

Donna is pragmatic, like most cops; she calls them as she sees them. "One thing I can tell you about being a female police officer; you have three choices of what you can be; a lesbian, a whore, or a white gal who messes with black guys, and you almost always screw your partner, according to others."

There is a large organized contingent of female police officers in the St. Louis Metropolitan Police Department. As I have stressed throughout this writing, these young police women come to the job to excel. They have a leader, Angela Coonce, who is a Major. She's smart, efficient, and dedicated, and she's a nice person (she purchases my books); not many male cops do.

Angela is referred to as the godmother of the group. Cops are brutal; they label individuals, and groups. But if an attractive, intelligent young female cop is labeled as a lesbian by a bunch of jealous male cops, it takes quid pro quo out of the picture.

Donna retired from the St. Louis Metropolitan Police Department and is presently employed by City Liquor Control as an agent. Major Angela Coonce is now the Chief of Police for Washington University.

Jenna continued, "I spent a week in the hospital; I had a severe liver laceration and internal bleeding; every rib on my left side was fractured in a couple of different places. My left forearm was fractured in six places; I had lacerations and road rash from my head to my lower leg. I went through emergency surgery for my arm where they fixed the breaks and fixed the ulna and the radius, with pins, plates, and screws. They had to operate on my arm again because bone fragments were left inside my arm where they rotted and prevented new bone growth."

"The day I was released from the hospital, homicide investigators demanded that I report to the homicide offices to give a statement. We were able to put them off for a couple of days with the help of doctors, but within a couple of days of being released, I was summoned to homicide."

"The homicide Dick asked me questions about the night of the accident. I didn't remember that night, and he didn't believe me. He looked at me and told me I was lying, saying I could pretend I didn't remember, but the truth would come out, and it would look better coming from me than coming out as part of an investigation."

"I was a mess and this interview was just the beginning of the crap the department put me through. As bad as the department treated me though, the officers around me were awesome; they took care of me and looked out for me every step of my recovery. This is one of the reasons I held on with the department, and I did try to make it work because I still wanted to be an officer. The department sucked; the people who worked for it did not."

"It was obvious they didn't want me anymore. When I made it back to full duty, they sent me back to the fourth district; I worked for a gal who said she didn't care who I was, she had no intention of treating me any different than the rest of her crew; (overheard by

Jenna) the first day back to work was excruciating. I wasn't looking for special treatment, but to hear this being said about me with the venom she said it was crushing."

"I have bounced around and transferred; only one of them was a requested transfer. I requested to be transferred out of the fourth district. I walked into work every day to a large framed picture of the car Mike and I were in the night of the accident, which crashed and burned to a crisp; alongside it was a memorandum Mike had previously written about the dangers of police vehicle pursuits. I saw it every day before going to roll call. I asked Captain Larry O'Toole if the picture could be moved, and he told me "To live with it". He saw it as a teaching tool for other officers."

"Not a day goes by that I don't think about that night, and Mike. I left the SLMPD at the end of 2005 and was unable to get hired by any other police department. The city was blackballing me. It took an attorney going to the city and threatening to sue before they stopped doing whatever they were doing that prevented me from getting a job with another department."

"I applied and was hired by the Chesterfield Police Department in 2007, then last year, 2021, I was hired by the Ballwin Police Department. I like it here, I'm treated well."

18

LEANN ROBERTSON

& THE CRAZY HANDCUFFED LADY

Leann, like most of the cute cop gals, had the unknown desire to be a cop. It's substantive, meaningful, and dangerous. The job is like a beautiful wild animal that seems benign while you are admiring it, so gentle that it makes the voyeur want to pet it. You love it and you are sure that it loves you back; go ahead, pet it.....

Leann lived in Rolla, Missouri. About a two-hour drive from the St. Louis Metropolitan area. She applied to several police departments in the Rolla vicinity, and then in 2002, she applied to the St. Louis County Police Department.

The pay was $20.000 a year more at St. Louis County; the county offered her a police officer position; she took it. After the academy, she continued to live in Rolla. She commuted, daily to north St. Louis County to the first precinct; the precinct where Joann Lipscomb was murdered. It was a dangerous and busy precinct. It was north city seeping into north county. It's where Joann Lipscomb was gunned down.

Leann loved it there. It was what true police work was about; locking up criminals. In an environment where danger lurks around every curve, the cops tend to look out for each other. It made the job more fun for Leann; she had friends and they were fighting crime together.

Leann was/is a competitive bodybuilder and she's gorgeous. In 2006 she fought a firefighter/police officer from Des Peres, Missouri in the Guns and Hoses annual cop/fireman boxing competitions. (Cops in Des Peres are firefighters and police officers.) Leann didn't win or lose. She lasted three tough rounds.

Leann had a degree in Criminal Justice and was working on a graduate degree in social work. That particular degree is usually detrimental to doing police work. Cops tend to think of the people they arrest as the enemy. In the old days of police work, the saying was, "we aren't social workers." Today that motto would be considered racist.

Leann had an aunt who was a cop in a rural town near Rolla; she was murdered on duty. The Chief of the St. Louis County Police Department contacted Leann's mother in Rolla. He advised her that he was transferring Leann out of the first police precinct, and placing her in a safer precinct.

Leann was transferred to Wildwood, a west county bedroom neighborhood where houses start at half a million. She was bored. She spent almost eight years at St. Louis County, and then resigned. Rolla offered her a police job, and she took it.

Female police officers, at times, are used for searching and conveying female prisoners, and their own prisoners. Prisoners who complain of an illness or injury must be taken to a nearby hospital for evaluation upon confinement.

Leann had received a radio assignment to a car wash in Rolla. The manager called the police because two customers who were using the vacuum at the business had been there for four hours vacuuming the same car; they were stoned on meth.

When Leann pulled up to the car wash, she recognized the female customer, Nicole Poston. Leann knew that Nicole had a meth problem and she had tried to help Nicole in the past. She also knew that Nicole was wanted for a parole violation and that she was going back to prison for the violation.

Leann asked the cop question, "What are you doing?"

Nicole said, "Vacuuming out our car, so what?"

The male with Nicole said, "There's worms in the car, and they're on my hands."

Leann did a computer check on Nicole and the probation violation popped up; she arrested Nicole, and since she knew her, and had tried to help her in the past, Leann handcuffed Nicole in the front instead of behind her back.

Nicole faked a seizure, which meant she would have to go to the hospital for a fit for confinement examination and she had taken her back to the Rolla police department in a police cruiser.

Leann drove into the Sally Port (where prisoners are removed from conveyance) and was walking the prisoner into the jail.

The prisoner, Nicole, somehow had slipped off her handcuffs. She had them in her hands and she adjusted them so that the cuffs could be used as a weapon, like brass knuckles.

Leann had been on her cellphone, trying to get some social work help for Nicole. Poston muttered, "I'm not going back to jail," and struck Leann with the steel handcuffs, first in the temple, which stunned Leann, and then she continued to strike Leann several times in the face and head. Officers watching on closed-circuit television came to Leann's aid and subdued Nicole Poston.

Leann was hospitalized and then advised to take a few days off and report back to duty. She had severe headaches and when she complained to the Urgent Care physician, she was advised to take aspirin and drink water.

She was on light-duty and worked the desk, and answered telephones inside of the station house.

Leann had dizzy spells and pain, and the Urgent Care Physicians weren't doing her any good. Leann's husband is a retired United States Military veteran; he took her to the Veterans Administration Hospital. After an examination by a neurologist, she was diagnosed with Traumatic Brain Injury (TMI).

She fought that injury and eventually went back to work. It was a long painful injury. Nicole Poston, was sentenced to life in prison for the attack on Leann. It was recorded on the closed-circuit surveillance system and played for the jury.

On July 13, 2021, Leann (who is now a corporal in the Rolla Police Department) was driving back from Jefferson City, Missouri in a Jeep, with Abigail Bowen, a Compass Health counselor. Leann is a Crisis Intervention Team member in Rolla. They were involved in a head-on accident on Highway 63 near Rolla.

A sixteen-year-old girl was driving an SUV, sideswiped a car, then hit the Jeep head-on. The sixteen-year-old girl was killed. The driver of the jeep, Abigail, and passenger, Leann were airlifted to a hospital in Columbia and listed in serious condition.

Leann's right hand was separated from her wrist, hanging by tendons; her hand and, wrist are badly broken. She is right-handed and off-duty on medical leave. She was asked to go to the pistol

range to qualify; she can't even open a door with her right hand.
Leann loves being a cop; she has no regrets.

19

DETECTIVE AGGIE & THE SHOELESS MAN

Aggie Santangelo, spunky, cute, outgoing, and smart is a city girl; ask her where she grew up and she responds, "Saint Joan of Arc Parish," as if everyone in the world knows where that is.

Like most city-dwellers, she was always in the vicinity of a city cop. People in the community know them, their names, who their parents are, and who they are married to, just the same as they knew who the bad kids are and do not allow their children to associate with them. Cops, crooks; they go hand in hand.

When the city cops were hiring, Aggie figured, "Why not?" She took the test, scored high, and was hired. She loved the job, from the police academy to the south patrol precinct, Aggie fell right into the groove. She had a child when she was eighteen, soon after she was hired by the police department. She got married and had another child.

She was always smiling and laughing and enjoying the cop job. She was a Field Training Officer, which meant she trained newly graduated recruits from the police academy when they are transferred to a district. It pays a little more and there are perks involved.

Cops who desire more money for vacations or new cars, or a bigger house, work a second job. Security work pays okay, but it's the same old bump and grind, fighting, rolling around on pavement, people in your face, daring you to take action, and secondary employers demanding more than the cop wants to give for an off-duty gig.

Aggie sold real estate and she was good at it. The years rolled by for Aggie and she was considering a move into an investigative job within the police department. She kept her ear to the ground waiting for her chance.

On a sunny Sunday morning, while on loan to the second district she was driving around in her old neighborhood and she observed a fellow sitting on a huge boulder under an overpass with no shoes. It was secluded and he was out of the ordinary, circumstances that get cops killed. Aggie stopped her police car and asked the guy what he was doing.

She told me that the guy looked like Charles Manson, the famous serial killer. His eyes were going round in circles, and Aggie told the radio dispatcher where she was and what she was doing. She said she'd advise if she needed an assist car.

Aggie exited the police car and conversed with the shoeless guy. He talked about killing vampires and other crazy stuff; Aggie patted him down and found a butterfly knife in his back pocket, which she confiscated.

She tried to get him to give her his name so she could run a wanted check on him. She figured he was a walk away from the State Mental Hospital nearby. Aggie keyed her radio and was attempting to speak into the microphone on her lapel to give information to the radio dispatcher.

The crazy man struck her with his fist on the right side of her face. The punch knocked her against the police car; he was on her trying to get to her gun. They fought and eventually went to the ground. He was still on top of her tearing at her holster.

There was a man working at a warehouse nearby and he observed Aggie talking with the shoeless man. He didn't watch them continuously but occasionally glanced toward the police car. On one such glance, he didn't see Aggie or the man. The crazy man was on top of Aggie pounding her and tearing at her holster. She was fighting for her life and losing.

The warehouseman ran over and pulled the crazy man off of Aggie. Aggie grabbed her pistol and pointed it at both men. The warehouseman stated, "I came over to help you," and Aggie concentrated on the man who had assaulted her. By that time, he was completely engaged in hallucinations stating that he was Jesus Christ, things that cops deal with frequently.

The radio dispatcher had heard the struggle because Aggie had keyed the radio trying to ask for help as she was being beaten. The dispatcher put out an officer in need of aid call and the location of Aggie.

Cops respond from everywhere for an officer in need of aid call. Aggie had help, and the responding cops arrested the crazy man. Aggie went to the hospital and was out of commission for several weeks. She could hardly walk and her face was so swollen she couldn't open her mouth.

Aggie was eventually transferred to the juvenile division; she worked as an investigator, a detective, plainclothes with a take-home car some of the time. It was a good job and she liked it. Retirement is always on the mind of city cops. The pension is good and it gets better the longer the cop stays on the job.

Rationalization makes us stay; we ponder trying something else, but being independent and free with a pension check coming in forces us to stay. Aggie did eighteen years as a juvenile unit detective.

When the politics within the city change the ethnicity of specialized units within the police department change. The juvenile unit became predominantly black; the city is more than fifty percent black, so it only makes sense to small-minded bureaucrats that investigators should be considered because of race.

A new black commander came to the unit. He verbally attacked Aggie from the beginning of his tenure. New commanders desire to have their friends working for them and partying with them. It's always been that way in the St. Louis Metropolitan Police Department.

Without cause, Aggie was transferred to a north city district, a uniform assignment that she did not want. She was still having flashbacks of the beating she took from the shoeless man.

Aggie was never one to take sick leave; she didn't report to her new assignment, she took sick leave and then took early retirement. She was just short of twenty-five years in the St. Louis Metropolitan Police Department. The black commander was recently fired from the department for double-dipping (working a second job while on duty). Karma's a bitch.

She owns and operates Café Dolce at Daggett and Marconi on the hill, a super neat coffee house. She's a happy gal. Aggie won!

20

MICHAEL BROWN SHOOTING

ANDRIA VM RETURNS

On August 9, 2014, Michael Brown, an eighteen-year-old black man was shot by a Ferguson, Missouri police officer, Darren Wilson. To seasoned cops, this was not an unusual occurrence. To black inhabitants of section eight housing, welfare, and hatred on both sides of the spectrum, it wasn't deemed unusual, either.

In the mid-seventies, apartment complexes were being built in North St. Louis County (NOCO) to the cops and residents. The land was available and cheap. Construction costs were minimal and the white masses were leaving the City of St. Louis in droves escaping crime and corruption from good old boy politics.

The concept was simple: build them with swimming pools, and tennis courts and build them cheap, just barely enough to pass St. Louis County building codes. It was the curse of north St. Louis County.

The original builders received huge tax breaks from local municipalities and from St. Louis County Government. Those tax breaks only last for about twenty years and then the owners must start paying regular taxes. The complexes go on the market and are easily sold, usually purchased by investment firms or conglomerates.

The bottom line is profit, which means full occupancy with people who will pay their rent. Section eight housing is the answer to profit in apartment living. Communities like Ferguson, Missouri, mostly white, middle-class, working communities, are instantly thrust into chaos when government housing enters their hometowns.

The cops resent the influx of crime; the property owners, residents, and business owners resent it also. The section eight apartment dwellers are angered at being resented and hated.

Canfield Green is the apartment complex built in Ferguson. Four hundred units of low-income housing. The is no swimming pool anymore. Gunshots are frequent and many people are afraid to leave their apartments. Michael Brown lived there.

He was six foot four and weighed 292 pounds. Police Officer Darren Wilson was six feet four and weighed 210. Michael Brown punched Officer Wilson and tried to take Wilson's gun away from him after Brown strong arm robbed a businessman just blocks away.

Brown was shot by Wilson, six times in the chest and head. He died on the scene and his body lay in the street for hours. It's cop and crook business; don't screw with the cops and you won't get shot is the mantra for survival in America.

But attitudes had been changing. The criminal was now being studied as to why he was a crook. Outside influences had been thrown into the cop/crook game. The cops had always been outnumbered in the game, but the political elite (who had always been in charge of cop behavior) were now supporting the crooks, possibly because they were also criminals hiding behind titles.

Officer Darren Wilson was investigated, probed, and any and all evidence was examined pertaining to the case. There was a Grand Jury investigation, and Darren Wilson was exonerated of all accusations of wrongdoing.

There were international reactions to the Ferguson shooting, China, Germany, Egypt, Iran, and Russia, all enemies of America and freedom commented negatively about the shooting of Michael Brown.

Amnesty International sent a team of human rights observers, trainers, and researchers to Ferguson. The USA Director of Amnesty International said, "The U.S cannot continue to allow those obligated and duty-bound to protect to become those who their community fears most."

There were mass protests in Ferguson. The press stirred the pot and every police officer in the region was involved in protecting property and lives in that little North St. Louis County municipality.

St. Louis City cops were assigned to the police lines; the female cops, many of who had been coddled and protected in their roles as city cops were there on the front line with their male counterparts.

The cops were spat upon, had projectiles thrown at them, intimidated, and cursed. The protestors were allowed to get in the cop's faces and threaten them and their families. They held the line.

I had been a cop for thirty-five years in the City of St. Louis; I had never been spat upon. In most cases, in the city, if a cop had a female partner and someone threatened her, spit on her, or even attempted to intimidate her just because she was a police officer, the male partner would beat the assailant unconscious. It's an unwritten law.

Andria VanMierlo had been at her Monsanto executive protection gig for about two years. She'd traveled to Hawaii, New York, San Francisco, Seattle, Copenhagen, Switzerland, Germany, The Baltic, Canada, several times. Executives travel in private air jets and live first class, and so did Andria.

She lived out of a suitcase and was always in a hotel, somewhere. She missed her husband and St. Louis, and she missed the St. Louis County Police Department. She was a champ there.

She was in a motel room in Iowa when she turned the television on to the national news. The Ferguson protests were the highlight of the news stations. Cops being humiliated, attacked, and ridiculed for doing their jobs was the delight of liberal news outlets.

Andria was humiliated when she observed her brothers and sisters on the front line being attacked and ordered not to retaliate. Professional protestors and criminals flooded Ferguson; their intent was to burn it to the ground, but they needed the backing of the liberal news.

Provocation of the front-line cops was the order of the day. If they could cause an incident wherein the cops overreacted, overreached their authority, and broke ranks, the protestors would have eliminated Ferguson. Business owners hired armed guards to sit on the roofs of their buildings with rifles aimed at the looters. The protestors didn't burn Ferguson down, but they looted, shot at cops, and stole and abused authority, and they got away with it.

The Missouri Highway Patrol was given the responsibility of supervising the cops on the front line. To the city cops, the thought of being supervised by Highway Patrol guys was laughable. City cops have been fighting the cop/crook war for a century while highway cops have been writing speeding tickets, but that's the way it went down.

Andria came into town the next day, had a day off, and sped to the St. Louis County Police Headquarters; she asked for her old job back. By the time she was hired the Ferguson protests were weaker but still going on. On the anniversary of the incident, the protests would start all over again, but she was happy to be back from her executive protection adventure. She was sent back to the fourth precinct on the island of Oakville.

The job of "law enforcement officer" was never the same after the Michael Brown shooting, protests, and riots. A city cop union executive, Jeff Roorda, dubbed it, The Ferguson Effect, and wrote a nonfiction book of the same name. Roughly analyzed and deciphered by a cop, it means that on the surface, cops were no longer able to protect and serve. In their minds, the public hates them; police stations in today's hatred-of-cops trend are like firehouses. Cops go out when they are called. They've always had to protect themselves, and their citizens against violent criminals, but they were now the victims. In many cities, cops were hunted, stalked, and ambushed.

Dial 911 in most major cities in the United States and you will be placed on hold. It was time for the citizens of America to handle their own emergencies.

But it goes deeper than that: Cops (majority) feel as if they are superheroes. Deep in their psyche, they realize they are working for politicians and they are protected by politicians. The judicial system is, was their friend, protecting them against frivolous attacks from the criminal masses who are roaming the streets of this country waiting for a chance to victimize hard-working God-fearing Americans. It's what keeps them together, mentally. Their purpose in life.

After Michael Brown, and when the regional cops were placed on the front line in Ferguson to be abused and ordered to not take action, the attitudes of cops changed as the system of justice in America changed.

When the riots subsided and the protests stopped, the cops went back to their departments with a different attitude. They no longer trusted the politicians or the judicial system. Cops were going to jail for doing their job; criminals were becoming the victims because the press and the weak knee politicians said so. The system had failed everyone, citizens, cops, hard-lined judges, and conservative prosecutors. The bad guys won.

At a roll call in the fourth precinct, Island of Oakville, a lieutenant watch commander gave a speech to his platoon before they went out into the night to protect and serve. It's cop tradition, unofficial and unmeaningful because the cops are going to do whatever they want to do.

There had been increased car break-ins at The South County Mall, the last bastion of shopping safety in the south county/south city area. The watch commander told his group to start doing car checks on black folks driving in or near the mall. An old cop supervisor (who was a one-time a City of St. Louis cop) took offense at the remark and wrote a scathing letter (anonymously) to internal affairs.

Cops have enemies: most of them are cops. An enemy of the watch commander with the quick lip was assigned to investigate the alleged allegation. The cops who were at roll-call were individually ordered to respond to internal affairs and questioned about the remark.

Cops don't have the luxury of being able to decline making a statement. If they don't comply, they are immediately fired. The inmates were running the asylum in the fourth precinct.

Greg VanMierlo was one of the cops at roll call. The watch commander was fired from the St. Louis County Police Department. Andria VanMierlo was still at Monsanto. Greg VanMierlo resigned from the county police department and was hired by the municipality of Des Peres, Missouri.

At about that same time, Andria was being stalked by a mental patient she had arrested a year or so earlier in Lemay, a little berg attached to Oakville at the north, (not on the island) separated by interstate highway 255. The guy was exposing himself to young children and offering them money.

Andria had been contacted by the mental patient (stalker) on Facebook after her full name appeared on a Facebook page of a bodybuilding contest promoter. The stalker apparently realized who she was and became infatuated with her, messaging her and attempting to converse with her.

Andria investigated the guy and found out he was under the care of a therapist in Poplar Bluff, Missouri. The stalking continued and Andria was granted an order of protection (ex parte) against him.

The Facebook messaging and the stalking continued. In August of 2017, the mental patient's therapist called Andria and warned her that the stalker said he was going to drive to St. Louis and go to Andria's residence in Oakville and that he was armed with a firearm.

Andria was scheduled to work that evening and her husband Greg was going to be at the house. At about 6:15 p.m. Greg heard his dogs going crazy, at the front door, jumping and barking.

Greg stated he looked out the window and observed the stalker looking in the window; the stalker was knocking on the door as he peered inside. Greg was afraid the stalker was going to try and break into the house.

Greg hit the emergency button on his cell phone to dial 911 and was put on hold by the emergency dispatcher; he put the phone on speaker and went outside via a sliding glass door to confront the stalker.

The stalker was inside his pickup truck in the driveway of the VanMierlo residence. Greg pistol paralyzed him and removed him from the truck, handcuffed him. and waited for St. Louis County police to arrive. A neighbor eventually recalled 911 and a dispatcher answered.

The stalker knew Greg's first name and he said, "Greg, you know I'm not violent, I'm Jesus." He said he was going to have thirty-four wives and Andria was going to be top-dog. The stalker was eventually placed in a state mental facility; Andria testified in a couple of confinement hearings; she and Greg hope the problem is over.

21

DETECTIVE TRENT KOPPEL, QUID PRO QUO

Trent grew up, for the first five years of her life, in Webster Groves, Missouri. It's the kind of place that television sitcoms are made in; perfect little houses, tree-lined streets, nice restaurants, and a vibrant shopping area.

She was a twin (sister) from a family that had ten kids and Trent was the second youngest. Her sister died at the age of three years, and six months. Trent's mother had a terrible resentment toward her because Trent reminded her of her twin sister. Trent felt she always had to prove herself to her mother. When she was a teenager, she realized her mother would never be happy with her, so she acted out. She shoplifted from malls, smoked weed, and did things she truly regrets. But she never got caught stealing or arrested for smoking weed.

Because Trent's sister died at such a young age, and because her mother hated the house they were living in, she decided to move the family to south St. Louis County. The rest of her life would be played out in south county (SOCO).

There was hardly any money in their family, and after her parents divorced (Trent was 16) they were really poor. She wore her brother's hand-me-downs, even his underwear; obviously, she hated the circumstances.

Trent would pretend (in high school) that she wasn't hungry at lunch just to hide the fact that she had no money for food, sometimes picking up food at the top of the trash cans in the cafeteria, which were right next to the restrooms. She used "going to the bathroom" as an excuse to reach in and grab something to eat as she walked by. She prayed no one would see her. She got her first part-time job when she was sixteen, shortly after her parents divorced. Being hungry and wanting nice clothing to wear made her work at her part-time job much harder.

Trent had an uncle who was a police officer in the City of St. Louis. He was a motorcycle cop. He was kind to Trent and he occasionally mentored her. She liked his uniform; he rode his motorcycle with a cigarette sticking out of his mouth. Trent thought that was cool.

Her uncle paid attention to Trent and told her she could be anything she wanted to be; because of that statement, Trent decided she wanted to be a police officer. At age sixteen she set her sights on police work.

She was married at 21 and gave birth shortly thereafter. She entered the St. Louis County Municipal police academy at age 24. Her uncle pinned her badge on her at the academy graduation. Municipal police academies were pay-as-you-go institutions. The graduating semi-cop has the responsibility to find their own jobs in law enforcement.

Trent chose police work because, in her life, she had done everything possible to align herself with the thought that she hated people; in reality, she had a soft spot in her psyche and she loved helping people. Making people happy made her happy.

Trent applied for and was hired by the City of Crestwood, Missouri. Crestwood was a small bedroom community in south St. Louis County until the early 60s when developers built the huge Crestwood Mall. Because of its location, it was an instant hit. The same thing happened in north St. Louis County with the building of Northwest Plaza, and Jamestown Mall. All three malls are now torn down. Crime shut them all down.

Trent worked for the Crestwood Police Department for six years. She was naive and cute with large breasts. She was a target for an older higher-ranking man. He was a captain with a bad marriage and he saw Trent as someone he could abuse.

He would fondle her breasts and her buttocks at will, and he did the same thing to two other female police officers. It was what old cops did to young female cops. A female cop friend once told me that every woman cop in the St. Louis Metropolitan Police

Department has been sexually harassed at some point in their employment. Quid pro quo is alive and well in law enforcement.

The sexual harassment was having a negative effect on Trent. She hated to go to work, and she was crying much of the time. She told her husband about the captain and her husband was going to go into the station and pummel him (he's a firefighter) but Trent told him not to. She was determined to be successful in her chosen field of endeavor.

Trent and the two other female Crestwood Police Officers sued the police department and the captain. They won the lawsuit but it was obvious her job in Crestwood would be ending. She had law enforcement experience and she had served honorably. She began applying to other police departments. The lawsuit followed her to every job she applied for, except for one, the Municipality of Des Peres, Missouri. She had been "that girl cop who sued Crestwood". Des Peres was another mall town; West County Mall is the focal point and the financial base of the city. She was hired by Des Peres.

Des Peres is a unique city and police department. The cops are firemen as well as cops, trained in both fields and EMT certified. Their duties are split in half; half of their days are firemen and half police work.

The West County Mall takes up much of their police duties. Retail theft is huge and with the "woke" generation prevailing at this point in history, groups of thieves enter a store and walk out with whatever they desire. A shopper can observe thieves walking through the door with the alarms on the items they have stolen hitting the blaring door alerts.

Trent had an interest in retail theft (she had been there) and she wanted to make a difference in her new cop lifestyle. Her friends from her youth would say to her, "You a cop? No way you are a cop".

She admits to being a shithead kid and she understood their disbelief in her career choice and she wanted to prove she was a different person, a better version of what she was and is. But in retrospect, she was the one who devised the nefarious plans, and they (the kids in school) were dumb enough to do what she told them to do and always seemed to get caught, but not Trent. She never got caught. She isn't proud of her behavior.

So, Trent worked for the City of Des Peres as a cop/firefighter, trained in both fields. Des Peres is the highest-paid police department in the region. The West County Mall was rebuilt in 2002 and she worked in the mall for the first five years, investigating fraud and retail theft. She was then transferred to the detective bureau and only occasionally she would have to ride the fire truck or the ambulance.

She was a supervisor with the Major Case Squad, the Public Affairs Officer (PIO) the evidence manager, and officer of the year twice, with four years of nominations. She was good at fraud and was a member of the Identity Theft Task Force. She was deputized as the Field Officer for the Secret Service and worked closely with them for ten years.

She was never allowed to be a part of the promotional process; that would mean she would have to be assigned to shift work, being a fireman schedule of two on, two off, three on, three off. She had two young kids at home at the time, both teenagers and they needed her, not to mention that her fireman husband had an opposing work schedule, and they had the typical cop wife, fireman hubs issues, and she wasn't going to allow her marriage to fail; cops are 60% likely to have failed marriages; firemen are 50%. In her mind that meant she was looking at a 110% possibility, that her marriage was in trouble.

Trent injured her shoulder while on duty; she was set to go to the fire academy and she ignored it so she could participate. Training to be a firefighter is strenuous, but she ignored the pain and worked through it. After graduating she went to a specialist who advised her the shoulder was dislocated. She had surgery to repair it; it's still painful.

In 2010 she earned her Master's Degree in criminal justice; she went immediately into teaching at St. Louis Community College, Meramec. After three years of teaching Trent began teaching at Maryville University. She became acquainted with Geri Brandt, The Director of the law enforcement studies department. She still teaches at Maryville; Evidence Recovery, Police Report Writing, Police Supervision, and Multicultural Policing.

Trent worked at Des Peres for 17 years. She met The Director of Security at Edward Jones investment Company while assigned to the Des Peres Detective Bureau. She was offered the position of Team Leader for the director's security staff. She accepted the position and quit Des Peres. In the beginning, she worked straight midnights.

Trent's been promoted three times; she is assigned to the Managing Partner of the company. Trent says her female boss is the best role model anyone could have (man or woman). She says what she means and means what she says. Trent is glued to her and loves her job.

Trent drives her, protects her, and flies with her on a private jet. Her female boss is a genuine person. No glimpses of falsehood; she makes Trent want to be the best she can be. Those feelings are not common in the cop job.

Trent's still married (28 years) the cop job didn't make her a statistic. Her children are grown and Trent's a happy former cop.

22

POLICE OFFICER BAILEY COLETTA

St. Louis cops have the reputation as shooters of the bad guy; since the city is over fifty percent black that equates to shooting the black guy. Jason Shockley, an educated and intelligent combat (Iraq war) veteran, applied to the St. Louis Police Department and was hired. He was quality meat for the department and the city. After the police academy, he hit the ground running in a north police district.

On 12-20-2011, Shockley and his partner observed what they thought was a drug deal going down behind a Church's Chicken. Jason was driving the cop car; they tried to stop the car Anthony Lamar Smith was driving and a pursuit began; the conversation between him and his partner was recorded by their body cameras; Shockley advised his partner that he was going to kill the driver of the car which eventually stopped.

Shockley approached the car and the driver Anthony Lamar Smith pointed a pistol at Shockley. Shockley shot him five times, killing him. The shooting was deemed justified; Shockley became disillusioned with the city and the police department and returned to the State of Texas to resume his life and try to forget his St. Louis experience.

Since Anthony Lamar Smith was black, it was safe for the black community to make the presumption that Police Officer Jason Shockley planted the gun on Smith after he shot him. That mindset isn't beyond the realm of reality in St. Louis.

The city prosecutor was presented with the fact that Shockley's DNA was found to be on the gun Anthony Lamar Smith presumably pointed at Jason Shockley. There were rumbles in the jungle over that evidence. Shockley hired an attorney. The logical explanation was that Shockley removed the gun from Smith's dead hands after he killed him. Made sense to the prosecutor.

Time rolled on. A new, black, woke prosecutor, Kim Gardner, was elected as the Circuit Attorney for the City of St. Louis, which is an island of violent behavior (murder capital of America) in a sea of professional sports teams. They and the Budweiser Brewery are the only ones who make any profits in this death burg, except for the city government.

Circuit Attorney Kim Gardner, who routinely has allowed felons to sidestep the scales of justice, decided to prosecute Jason Shockley for the murder of Anthony Lamar Smith. A grand jury indictment allowed her to have Jason Shockley returned to St. Louis, booked for murder, and released on bond.

Jason Shockley was not judged by a jury of his peers. A white man, a cop, has no peers in the City of St. Louis. There was a bench trial, meaning that the presiding judge would determine guilt or innocence.

After all was said and done, Kim Gardner lost the trial and Jason Shockley walked away a free man. He headed back to the safe State of Texas. But the black masses in the City of St. Louis were angry. They were stirred up previously by the Michael Brown police killing in Ferguson, Missouri.

Professional protesters again flocked to the St. Louis region. Most were/are criminals hiding behind the protestor moniker. Massive violent protests erupted. The leaders in the St. Louis Metropolitan Police Department (most of which had always had desk jobs) weren't familiar with massive protests.

They instructed their troops to hold the line, kettle the protestors, and arrest them. An undercover black cop, a guy who everyone liked, was placed in the belly of the mobs of criminals to document and at times videotape what was happening, possibly for future prosecution.

Whoever had that idea misinterpreted the abilities of Luther Hall. The city was a warzone, a battleground for white cops and black criminals. The sacrificial cop, Luther Hall, wasn't a warrior he was a nice guy. He was out of his element. The cops were wrought up and out of control. They were angry and led to believe they were protecting their city and would be rewarded in the future by the Commissioner and his minions who watched the combat from their fifth-floor windows of police headquarters.

Luther Hall, the cop everyone liked, got beat up by some white cops. It wasn't an unusual beating, not as violent as Rodney King in Los Angeles, it was the kind of beating city cops give to errant black men. They didn't know Luther Hall was the fatted calf who had been thrown out into the jungle to be slaughtered.

When the protests subsided and the dust settled, the federal investigations began. There were videos by news stations, and the beating of Luther Hall was on tape. The FBI began interviewing city cops. A federal Grand Jury subpoenaed several cops.

All in all, four cops were interviewed and indicted. Several lied to the FBI, 18 USC 1001, a few went to prison. Luther Hall sued the police department and got rich. One of the cops, Randy Hays, was sentenced to 51 months in prison for the beating of Luther Hall.

Randy Hays's girlfriend, Police Officer Bailey Coletta, was present at the beating. She was interviewed by the FBI; she lied to them. She went before a Federal Grand Jury and she lied to them. Cops don't understand federal investigations; the FBI knows the answer to the questions they are asking before they ask them. They want you to lie.

The Assistant United States Attorney knows the answer to the questions the cop is going to be asked before they ask it, and they advise the seated grand jurors of such. They are waiting for you to lie so they can indict you.

There were many victims involved in the Jason Shockley acquittal protests. Bailey Coletta is just one of them. She was a local girl, cute and considerate who wanted more out of life than being an office worker in some downtown company, so she joined the police department.

It is exciting, and there is peer pressure involved. Lying cops are rationalizing their way into the federal prison system. Bailey Coletta pled guilty and lost her cop job. She was one of the lucky ones. She had to spend a short stay in federal prison. Peer pressure is a bitch.

23

POLICE OFFICER KATLYN ALIX

THE NEGATIVE ASPECT OF POWER

Beauty is power; particularly in a business where the employee is the product of the company. Cops are the product of the city they are employed by, there is no other product, not crime statistics, arrest stats, or work ethic.

A beautiful woman within the ranks of the St. Louis Metropolitan Police Department is treated differently than the average cop. The male cop supervisors dote on them, counsel them, give them special assignments and partners who will protect them, and secretly imagine being alone with them. Hair of the dog. Their male partners take the role of protector and the eight-hour stint in a police car is in reality, date night.

Katlyn Alix was a beautiful woman. She was a military veteran, deployed to Guantanamo Bay Cuba to work as a prison guard, and graduated from the St. Louis Metropolitan Police Department in January of 2017. She was sent to the sixth police district in north St. Louis. It is a predominantly black district, but at one time was a middle-class section of the city where businesses and working-class families thrived.

Walnut Park was a vibrant neighborhood in the late 60s, but the failed federal government high-rise housing projects in the city were evacuated and torn down leaving neighborhoods like Walnut Park in the crosshairs of HUD.

Working class families sold their homes and evacuated to Spanish Lake in North St. Louis County. Most folks who work for a living only have their homes. Very few have savings.

Katlyn paid her dues in the sixth police district and was eventually moved to the second police district. It is the only district in the City of St. Louis that has a low crime rate. She married another cop, Tony Meyers, which is dicey in the cop job. If married cops are on different recreation schedules, they barely see each other. The cop's job is the romantic partner.

The new recruit is overwhelmed by the job of a police officer in a big city. The job tricks the young cop into believing he/she is special. The power given to the new cop by the State of Missouri is breathtaking. The job matters more than anything else in their lives, family, religion, or marriage.

The carrying of the gun is in itself overwhelming. The wearing of the badge equals that experience. For the new cop, camaraderie plays big. In the police academy, it is all that matters. The cop recruits rely on each other; they help cops who are slow in any aspect of performance, test-taking, or physical ability. Strong friendships are developed there, but they hardly last. The cops are spread out after graduation and hardly ever see each other. So many cops resign, get fired, or die.

Police Officer Nathaniel Hendren was a seven-year veteran of the department and was assigned to the second police district. He and Katlyn were partners frequently. Nathaniel Hendren is an impressive guy. He graduated magna cum laude from college and was number two in his academy class, and was a former Marine. He was overqualified to be a cop.

A romance blossomed between them, even though Katlyn was married, actually a newly-wed, three months into their marriage; that fact did not sway her; Nathaniel Hendren was not concerned about being romantically involved with a fellow cop's wife. The moral values were/are shallow in a cop/cop romance. They had the mantra; you can do whatever you like.

In a roundabout way, cops are trained that they are special people and that the power they yield over crooks and not-so-crooked citizens of the city they are serving is discretionary.

Protecting yourself at all times is the cop recruit mantra; do whatever you want to do. The badge says, St. Louis Metropolitan Police Officer. The cop does whatever he feels should be done at the time of his engagement with the citizens of his/her city.

When I was a young cop, the mantra was different. A training officer would advise the recruit that the badge said St. Louis

Metropolitan Police Officer and that you can do whatever you want as long as you can write your way out of trouble.

The power of the police experience guides us through the maze of police work. It controls us and gives us false beliefs about the judicial system. The gun, the badge, and the mantra are not there to help the cop, it is there to keep him/her infatuated enough to continue to show up for work and do the dirty business of the agency they're employed by.

The problem with the mantra is that the cop doesn't leave it at work. It follows him home like a stray dog or a vengeful rattler.

On January 24, 2019, Nathaniel Hendren was on the night-watch with his other partner, Patrick Riordan in the second police district. Katlyn Alix was off duty. The night watch had just begun for Hendren and Riordan. At 11:18 p.m. Katlyn Alix sent Hendren a text message stating, "Hi, I'm happy, let's hang out."

Hendren replied, "Come see me."

Hendren and his partner drove to 700 Dover Street, which is in the first police district, Hendren's apartment, and Katlyn was already there. During that time Hendren and Riordan received a radio assignment for an alarm sounding in their district; they didn't respond to it.

When Alix and Hendren entered Hendren's apartment, Hendren admitted that he drank some alcohol and that Alix also drank alcohol. Most cops carry two guns with them. The police department's nine-millimeter Beretta is big and cumbersome and if someone knows what they are doing they can disarm a cop and kill them with their own gun.

Revolvers are usually carried in the cop's pocket, small and concealable, and always ready to fire, they're backup weapons. Cops, especially young cops play with their guns. It's the magic machine that makes them strong, smart, powerful, and invincible. Hendren was wearing a bulletproof vest; Alix was not. She was in civilian clothing.

Hendren admitted to taking out his off-duty revolver, he said Alix was the first person to show a weapon that night. Hendrin and Alix were taking turns firing at each other with Hendren's weapon which had a single bullet in its cylinder. Each fired the weapon once. The second time Hendren fired it, the gun discharged. The bullet struck Alix in the chest.

After Alix was hit, Hendren and Riordan attempted to perform first aid and transport her to SLU Hospital. Apparently, Hendren dropped Alix multiple times; he had difficulty putting her in the backseat of his police vehicle.

Shortly before 1:00 a.m., Alix, Hendren, and Riordan arrived at SLU Hospital. Alix's shirt had been removed, and her sports bra was pulled over her head. Hendren said that happened because of "lifesaving efforts in the vehicle on the way to the hospital." She was DOA.

Hendren was charged with involuntary manslaughter. He made statements that he was in love with Katlyn Alix, and they were going to move in together. He pled guilty to the charge and was sentenced to seven years in the Missouri State Penitentiary. Beauty was destroyed.

I was a City of St. Louis cop for 35 years. A detective and street cop, never a supervisor who sat in an office and judged the cops fighting the war on the street, the stationhouse, the courtroom, and in their own homes. I had never seen such a bizarre case of gut-wrenching sadness as the Katlyn Alix death.

But the beat goes on in the cop/crook game. Go into one of the three district super stations and mention the name, Katlyn Alix, and no one would even know who or what you were talking about. History is moot; the past doesn't exist; only the belief in immortality.

24

BEAU ROTHWELL, MURDERER

MEETS SGT. ANDRIA VM

Beau Rothwell, a chemical engineer, married to a college friend and lover, Jennifer, who was also a chemical engineer living in upper-middle-class Creve Coeur, was having an affair with another woman. Most men and women can justify infidelity but it is actually the beginning of the end.

Beau and Jennifer were trying to get pregnant. It became a chore for Beau; a reasonable excuse for murder? Beau thought so. On November 11, 2019, he and Jennifer fought, verbally at first, and then Beau lost his temper, grabbed a wooden mallet, and struck Jennifer in the head numerous times fracturing her skull and causing her to fall down the basement steps. She had just advised Beau that she was pregnant. Jennifer was dead.

Beau went into panic mode believing he had to hide and fix the situation. He went to different stores and purchased cleaning supplies, using cash and gift cards. Around 2:00 in the morning he decided he need to remove the body from the house. He grabbed a tarp and moved Jennifer's body to his pickup truck.

He had seen crime shows on television where the killer sometimes removes the clothing of the victim so he stripped Jennifer's lifeless body and put a bag over her head. He drove out of town and did not know where he was going; he said he drove until he was lost. He dumped her body in a field and covered it with some grass and branches.

The next day Beau drove Jennifer's car down Olive Boulevard and ran it off the road so it looked like she got into a crash, He walked back home and went to work himself. He called 911 at 9:44 p.m. that night to report his wife missing, saying he last saw her that morning as she was leaving for work.

Obviously, the cops didn't believe Beau. St. Louis County Homicide was called in to take the case. County and Creve Coeur police searched the wooded area around the house in Creve Coeur.

Sergeant Andria VanMierlo was the supervisor of the Special Response Unit based in north St. Louis County. She and her unit were requested to help with the search of the wooded area around the Rothwell home. Their search was to no avail, but Andria noticed that there was one trash can sitting at the curb of the Rothwell home and that none of the neighbors had their trash cans out.

She asked for permission from County Homicide to search the trash can. She got it and her team did a "trash pull". They found receipts from the purchase of cleaning products, bleach, and other chemicals used to clean blood.

Andria gave them to homicide. The receipts provided probable cause to obtain a search warrant to search the Rothwell residence. County and Creve Coeur detectives found blood and bleach-soaked carpeting while searching the home. Rothwell led them to her body in some woods about an hour away.

Beau Rothwell was sentenced to life in prison without the possibility of parole. Andria VanMierlo resumed her duties in north St. Louis County with little fanfare. But her ideology of law enforcement was waning. The job had changed. Catching the bad guy was now in jeopardy; in many instances, the cop was deemed the bad guy.

In the eyes of cops, the world had been turned upside down. Cops were going to work wondering if they were going to survive their shift without being arrested, or placing themselves in a position of being later indicted for something they had done daily in the past.

On March 2, 2022, Andria VanMierlo again resigned from the St. Louis County Police Department. Her almost twenty years of service, sacrifice, and dedication will provide her with a meager pension somewhere down the line, maybe when she's 60 years old.

Will her unselfish unrelenting enthusiasm be missed? No! But Andria is a positive person, a thinker, and a worker. She now runs a fitness and personal training company on the island of Oakville

Andria has a saying, "I can't be beaten, I will win."

25

Captain David Dorn

Sergeant Ann Dorn

On May 25, 2020, in Minneapolis, Minnesota a career criminal, George Floyd, a black man, purchased a pack of cigarettes with a counterfeit twenty-dollar bill. The store owner called 911 and police officer Derek Chauvin was given the call. Two other police officers were given the assist, J. Alexander Kueng and Thomas Lane.

George Floyd was sitting in a car parked near the store. The officers approached him and requested he exit the vehicle, and after exiting the officers attempted to handcuff him. Lane pointed a gun at Floyd's head prior to the handcuffing. A fourth police officer, Tou Thao, prevented bystanders from intervening and Floyd was taken to the ground.

Officer Chauvin knelt on Floyd's neck in an attempt to restrain him. Prior to being placed on the ground, Floyd had exhibited signs of anxiety, he complained about being claustrophobic and being unable to breathe.

Floyd became more distressed and officer Chauvin continued to kneel on his neck still trying to restrain him. Floyd begged for Chauvin to stop kneeling on his neck. After several minutes, Floyd stopped speaking.

Officer Kueng checked his pulse when urged to by bystanders. Chauvin ignored pleas from bystanders to lift his knee from Floyd's neck. Floyd ultimately died at the scene of his arrest.

The liberal populace of Minneapolis was enraged; the liberal press in the nation began the spin on the accidental death of criminal George Floyd.

Derek Chauvin didn't come to work with murder in his heart; he was doing what all cops do or have done for the past 100 years; stop cause for further complaint. Subdue the arrested subject and try not to get hurt in the process.

The press screamed that Floyd's death was systemic racism. It was the battle cry for professional protestors to hit the streets in every major city in the United States. Professional protestors are professional criminals.

They are ensconced in every major city in the United States because every major city is democratic controlled and primarily black.

Wealthy communist rabble rousers tossed millions of dollars into a group called Black Lives Matter. It is now a wealthy anti American socialist controlled group of protestors. On June 2, 2020, St. Louis was hit with the rioters.

Downtown St. Louis became a warzone. A 711 Convenience Store with a police substation (as was previously described in this writing) was burned to the ground.

The chief of police was crying on camera, begging for the rioters to stop the carnage. The rioters continued through the night. The gangs moved westward, and eventually found their way to Lee's Pawn Shop on Dr. Martin Luther King Boulevard.

It was near the house David and Ann Dorn lived in. It was an all-black part of the city and David had lived there with his first wife; he raised his children in that house.

David was retired from the St. Louis Metropolitan police Department but had taken the job of Police Chief in a small north county community.

David Dorn saw himself as a super hero for the down trodden of the world. He was well respected and liked by both sides of the spectrum.

David Dorn, a career police officer had helped more people than he had arrested in his profession. He was close friends with the pawnshop owner and he had answered the alarm soundings at the pawnshop for thirty years. They were mostly false alarms. Dave would go to the shop, look for any signs of burglary, and then go back home and go to bed.

On this deadly night, Dave climbed out of bed and didn't advise Ann that he was going to check on the pawnshop. She would have asked to go with him and Dave didn't think he needed her.

Although, the alarm company advised Dave that the front door of the pawnshop had been breached. He arrived at the pawnshop and he confronted a few rioters outside, one of whom was a man named Stephan Cannon.

David told them it wasn't worth it, that there was little of value in the shop that wasn't tightly locked up. Moments later Cannon shot David in the chest. He bled out on the sidewalk; a third rioter live-streamed the entire incident, and one of the viewers who watched Dave's murder unfold was Dave's eldest grandson.

Cannon was found guilty of first-degree murder.

Ann Dorn met her future husband while working retail security, David Dorn moonlighted at the same store. David was black; Ann is white. They became friends, and that friendship eventually blossomed into love.

After sixteen years together, they were finally married for another fourteen years, married on a beach in Jamaica.

Dave was a charismatic guy. He loved police work and he loved the St. Louis Metropolitan police Department. Life was good for he and Ann.

Ann spoke at the 2020 Republican National Convention. She is a rightwing law and order conservative. She blamed the Black Lives Matter movement and other progressive activists such as Vice President Kamala Harris for dividing America, blasting them as supervillains.

Ann Dorn is white, but she's blacker than Kamala Harris. There's a thin line between a white St. Louis cop and a black St. Louis resident.

Now Ann is alone.

Made in the USA
Columbia, SC
09 February 2023

11548339R00100